MASTERING CHARACTER *ARCS*

MASTERING CHARACTER ARCS

HOW FIFTEEN UNIVERSAL JOURNEYS CAN POWER UP YOUR NOVEL'S CAST

LEWIS JORSTAD

Mastering Character Arcs: How Fifteen Universal Journeys Can Power Up Your Novel's Cast

The Writer's Craft Series — Book Two

Published by The Novel Smithy, LLC.

Printed in the United States of America.

1st Edition, 2022

ISBN (print): 978-1-955157-06-3

ISBN (digital): 978-1-955157-07-0

ISBN (hardcover): 978-1-955157-08-7

https://thenovelsmithy.com/

❀ Created with Vellum

The Ten Day Novelist Series

The Ten Day Outline
The Ten Day Draft
The Ten Day Edit
The Ten Day Author

The Writer's Craft Series

Write Your Hero
Mastering Character Arcs

CONTENTS

JOIN THE LIBRARY!

Ever wish there was a library of resources built just for novelists? Well, guess what—there is!

Check out the **Novel Smithy Resource Library** and grab your **FREE Character Creation Workbook**.

https://thenovelsmithy.com/library/

WRITING IN LAYERS

One of my favorite exchanges in any movie comes, oddly enough, from *Shrek*:

Shrek: Ogres are like onions. [...]

Donkey: If you leave them out in the sun, they turn brown and start sprouting little white hairs?

Shrek: No! Onions have layers! Ogres have layers!

Now, you might be wondering—am I seriously referencing a movie about a green ogre and his donkey companion in this book on character development?

And yes, yes I am.

You see, your characters aren't unlike Shrek. Not only will they face intense conflicts, get into trouble, and perhaps even fall in love, but they'll also have layers. These layers will come up again and again, no matter where you look. Your character's backstory will layer with their identity, creating a believable foundation for who they are. Their major turning points will layer with your plot, sparking powerful moments of no return throughout your novel. Even your cast will have layers, with each of your characters shaping (and being shaped by) the people around them.

Basically, everything about characters is built through layers —and that's equally true for your characters' arcs.

This is a potentially unusual take. Many writers think of arcs as a singular journey from point A to B. Your characters might grow and learn or decay and fail, but the rest is largely open ended. Whatever wild and wacky challenges your characters face have little bearing on their arc itself, so long as their final outcome remains the same.

However, I'm not sure this is true.

Over the years, I've studied a lot of arcs, from classics like the positive and negative arc, to the hero's arc and redemption arc. Though I'm certainly not the only one to find this, what I've discovered is that arcs don't exist in isolation—again, they form layers! Rather than having a lonely positive arc, many characters also follow additional arcs that add nuance and spice to their journey. These "secondary" arcs are the domain of hermits, rogues, lovers, and elders. They're full of variety, and also full of useful patterns we can use to write even better characters.

That's where this book arrives on the scene.

Over the next nineteen chapters, I plan to introduce you to fifteen character arcs, each uniquely suited for different members of your cast. Whether you're writing a heart-pounding crime thriller or a peaceful beach read, these arcs will serve as a framework for crafting engaging characters, equipping you with the tools you need to write deeply impactful stories.

To that end, this book will be organized in a series of short chapters, each focused on a specific element of successful character arcs. We'll start by laying some groundwork, exploring all the pieces needed to trigger your character's journey. From there we'll delve into each arc individually, their uses and quirks, as well as any pitfalls you might face. And finally, we'll wrap things up by bringing what you've learned together! From layering arcs into powerful combos to using archetypes to expand your cast, these new tools will affect nearly every aspect of your novel.

Though these layers may sound intimidating now, I promise you—by the time we're done, they'll be a wonderful asset in your writing journey. So, put on some music, grab a notebook, and let's get to work.

It seems Shrek had the right idea all along!

YOUR QUESTIONS

What can I expect from this book?

This book is organized in a series of short chapters, each focused on one part of writing a vibrant cast. Alongside their main topic, these chapters will include two key components:

- **Wrap-Up Questions:** At the end of each chapter, I'll ask you a handful of questions to help you apply everything you've learned to your cast. I highly recommend reflecting on these questions and saving your answers in either a notebook or outline. This way, by the time you've finished this book, you'll have not only gained the skills you need to write better arcs but also created a tangible document you can use to put that knowledge into action.
- **Case Studies:** Throughout this book, you'll also find a variety of case studies. These are in-depth explorations of popular stories, meant to show you what well-written characters look like in practice.

What examples will you use in the case studies?

Here's a complete list of the examples we'll use throughout this book:

- *The Hunger Games* (2008)
- *Legally Blonde* (2001)
- *The Godfather* (1972)
- *Nausicaä of the Valley of the Wind* (1984)
- *Shane* (1953)
- *Princess Mononoke* (1997)
- *Whale Rider* (2002)
- *Treasure Planet* (2002)
- *The Matrix* (1999)
- *Casablanca* (1942)
- *Sinbad: Legend of the Seven Seas* (2003)
- *It Happened One Night* (1934)
- *The Sound of Music* (1965)
- *Red River* (1948)
- *Star Wars: A New Hope* (1977)
- *My Fair Lady* (1964)
- *Avatar: The Last Airbender* (2005)
- *The Lord of the Rings* (1968)

Alongside these books and films, I'll also mention a few other stories, but only in passing. These examples will be our primary focus.

Why are most of these case studies focused on movies rather than books?

Though this book is geared towards novelists first and foremost, movies are simply a better fit for these case studies. This is because movies are far more approachable than novels. While I've aimed to pick films that most people will recognize, you can easily watch any of the movies mentioned in this book in an afternoon if necessary. In contrast, novels are a much larger time commitment—and therefore harder to use in this context.

What if I'm writing a series?

If you're planning to write a series of novels, everything you learn in this book will still apply. The only difference will be how your character arcs play out. Rather than completing their transformation in a single book, your cast will likely evolve over a range of novels. So long as you keep this in mind while reading, you should be just fine!

Do I need a finished first draft to benefit from this book?

Not at all!

If you do have a finished draft to work from, that's great, but it also isn't a requirement. Even if you only have a basic idea of what your story will look like, this book will still go a long way towards helping you better understand your novel's characters.

Do I need to read the other books in this series before I can start this one?

No—though it certainly wouldn't hurt!

I've tried to write this book so that it stands on its own, regardless of whether you've read the rest of The Writer's Craft Series. With that said, for those of you who have read *Write Your Hero,* this does mean you'll run into a few familiar topics, especially in Part One. This book expands on a lot of the concepts I didn't have space for in *Write Your Hero,* so there are definitely common themes running throughout both books.

What if I'm a total beginner? What about a more advanced writer?

This book is meant to be approachable (and useful) regardless of your skill level.

If you're new to the writing craft, earlier chapters will ease you into important topics so we can expand on them later on. Meanwhile, if you're more experienced, you may see some topics you're already familiar with—feel free to skim through those chapters for a quick refresher. As we progress deeper into the book, the topics we address will grow more complex!

1

BUILDING THEIR FOUNDATION

"Reading is an exercise in empathy; an exercise in walking in someone else's shoes for a while."

MALORIE BLACKMAN, BRITISH NOVELIST AND SCREENWRITER

1

IT'S ALL ABOUT CHANGE

For just a moment, I want you to imagine your favorite fictional characters.

Who are they? What do you remember about them? Why did they leave such a lasting impact?

While these questions might seem simple at first glance, your answers should reveal a lot about what makes for a well-written character. If you're anything like I am, your favorites run the gamut from all-powerful superheroes to noble princesses, warriors in disguise, and gentle lovers. On the surface, these don't have a lot in common—yet they all occupy the same place in our minds.

So, what connects these seemingly unrelated characters?

Well, in all likelihood, you love these characters not just because they're powerful, clever, or cool, but because they struggled for something meaningful. They faced failure, challenge, and hardship, and eventually learned important lessons that shaped the outcome of their story.

These types of journeys are easy to relate to. Throughout our lives, we'll all struggle to achieve our goals, get kicked down, and have to make the difficult choice to rise back up again. Perhaps you're coming of age and finding your footing in the adult world, or maybe you're cautiously returning to a community that once hurt you. You could even be facing conflict within yourself as you fight to come to terms with who you are and what legacy you want to leave behind.

Whatever these struggles are, they'll all follow a similar pattern of conflict, learning, and change. It's this pattern that links all of your favorite characters together, no matter how different they may seem—because it's this pattern that forms the foundation of their character arcs.

What Are Character Arcs?

Character arcs are a huge topic in the writing world, and for good reason. Not only are arcs integral to writing a dynamic, engaging cast, but they're also a useful tool for better understanding the story you're trying to write in the first place.

Here's a quick definition:

"A character arc is the internal transformation of a character as they struggle to overcome major flaws or wounds."

In layman's terms, this means character arcs are a framework, built on universal patterns that all stories share.

Your character will start your novel suffering from some internal problem, before setting their sights on a goal they hope will solve that problem. Along the way, they'll face challenges and obstacles, which will force them to learn important lessons that change who they are as a person. By the time this is complete, they'll have experienced a meaningful transformation, "arcing" from one place to another.

If you're used to other writing frameworks such as story structure, this should sound familiar. Just like structures such as the Three Act Structure help writers pace their plots through carefully crafted story beats, character arcs ensure your cast evolves organically thanks to a series of crossroads. After all, no character changes willingly! These crossroads are there to guide their journey, testing their progress and forcing them to learn despite their reservations.

This means arcs affect your novel in three big ways:

- **Your Cast:** Arcs help you create dynamic characters that feel alive and genuine. They also help you plan your cast. Between complimentary arcs, foils, and supporting archetypes, this is an excellent way to build a balanced, rich cast of characters.
- **Your Plot:** Character arcs are an important tool for weaving your plot and cast together. The crossroads in a well-written arc will naturally align with the major turning points of your plot, packing a nice double dose of impact for your readers. This is something we'll be returning to later in Part Four.
- **Your Readers:** Finally, arcs help readers identify with your cast. We've all experienced periods of transition in our lives, which means arcs are easy to relate to. When done well, this results in characters your readers actually want to stick around for.

With that said, slapping some basic transformation on your character and calling it an arc isn't quite enough. Character arcs aren't simply minor changes or shifts in perspective. Instead, well-written arcs require a few specific things:

- The character needs a strong motivation driving them forward
- Their journey needs a clear beginning and end
- There needs to be consequences if the character fails
- They should experience powerful turning points throughout their arc
- And this should culminate in some meaningful, lasting change

These elements come together to create something called *catharsis.*

Catharsis is a Greek term originally coined by Aristotle that describes the emotional release you feel at the end of a good story. After spending so long invested in a character's life, it's satisfying to see that adventure conclude. This is why you feel energized after watching a great movie or finishing a fantastic novel. These stories build up emotional tension and then release that tension at all the right moments.

Of course, to create this tension, you first need something worth getting invested in. This investment is created through three, relatively simple components, all of which rely in part on your characters:

- Change
- Failure
- Timing

I've mentioned change already, but it really is critical to writing a dynamic cast! Change is the secret spice that makes your characters feel alive and is thus a major focus of their arcs. Alongside this change, each of your characters will also pursue some goal, but they won't always get that goal right. These mistakes and failures will go a long way towards teaching them the lessons of their story, and towards giving your readers something to root for.

Meanwhile, catharsis requires careful timing. You'll need evenly paced turning points to keep readers invested in your story, as well as a balance between failure, success, resistance, and change. This is where arcs become so useful. Because character arcs build on common patterns, they provide the perfect blueprint for timing these elements, resulting in a cast of characters your readers can't help but get invested in!

Lessons from Chapter One

So, where do we go from here?

Well, the point of this book is to equip you with the knowledge you need to not only use character arcs, but understand them. Though all arcs are based on a similar framework, there are actually a variety of different arcs out there, from more general primary arcs to specialized secondary arcs.

Primary arcs can apply to any character in your novel, and are all about shaping their overarching transformation—while secondary arcs are optional arcs, meant to help you craft specific types of characters such as heroines, elders, or chosen ones. When combined, this gives you a ton of options, ensuring you can always find the perfect arc regardless of whether you're writing a gritty space adventure or a cozy beach romance.

However, I'm getting ahead of myself.

Before we can dive into the many types of character arcs (or how to turn those arcs into a cohesive cast) we first need to lay some groundwork. There are a handful of elements that successful arcs require, from powerful inner struggles to important lessons, motivations, identities, and more. These elements will form the foundation for every character you write—so, before we delve into arcs themselves, we better start by gathering our tools!

In the meantime, here are a few questions to help you apply what you've learned to your cast:

- How would you describe your character's story in a few sentences?
- What failures will they experience along the way?
- How do they evolve and change as their journey unfolds?
- How do these changes affect them and the world around them?

Once you've answered these questions, I'll see you in Chapter Two!

2

GATHERING THE PIECES

Conflict stands at the core of every good novel, but many writers assume "conflict" is limited to their plot. Explosions, car crashes, bar fights, and arguments are all easy forms of conflict to visualize, and thus the first thing our minds jump to when we start writing.

However, conflict goes far beyond these physical obstacles.

Alongside external forms of conflict, the best stories also include powerful internal conflicts. From the fear of change to the struggle to let go of the past, your novel will feature a variety of storms brewing within your characters. It's this internal conflict that provides the main fuel for your characters' arcs, forming a critical piece of the writing puzzle.

So, in this chapter, let's take a quick detour to explore all the things you'll need to craft character arcs of your own!

NOTE: This is a topic I explored at length in the first book of this series, *Write Your Hero,* so I plan to keep this chapter brief. Still, this topic is worth revisiting, even if you're already familiar with *Write Your Hero*—and for those of you jumping in for the first time, it's vital to understanding your cast.

The Building Blocks of Arcs

Like it or not, character arcs don't appear out of thin air!

Like so many aspects of writing a novel, arcs are built on a variety of important components. These components are what make your characters who they are, and include everything from their flaws to their history and perspective. When combined, these are what create the kinds of rich internal conflicts that lead to interesting journeys of change.

Of course, "flaws" and "history" are both a bit vague.

We'll explore those in more depth in just a moment, but for now, let's start with two specific terms you'll need to know:

- **Their Inner Struggle:** A harmful belief that holds your character back throughout your story. Sometimes called their lie or wound, this belief prevents them from achieving their goals and resolving the core conflict of your novel.
- **Their Truth:** The lesson your character needs to learn in order to overcome their inner struggle. This stands in direct contrast to their harmful beliefs, making this truth the "message" of their story. Accepting their truth is the final test of their arc.

These two elements will be at odds for most of your story, laying the groundwork for your character's internal conflict.

Their inner struggle is particularly important, because this sets the stage for their eventual transformation. This is not simply a character flaw, and is instead a deeply rooted belief that rests at the core of your character. While their flaw might be impatience or cowardice, their inner struggle will be harder to overcome:

- Submissive —> "I'm not worthy of others' respect. I'm lucky they talk to me at all."
- Cowardly —> "The world is dangerous. It's not safe for me to leave home."
- Aggressive —> "People are cruel. If I don't strike first, they'll hurt me instead."
- Demanding —> "I'm superior to others. I deserve their undivided attention."
- Self-Righteous —> "Only I know what's right. There's nothing I can learn from other people."

Meanwhile, their truth opposes these beliefs:

- Confident —> "I'm worthy of respect. It's ok to stand up for myself."
- Adventurous —> "I can take care of myself. I'm allowed to take risks."
- Trusting —> "Most people are kind. I don't need to fear them."
- Respectful —> "Everyone is equal. I'm grateful when people make time for me."
- Inquisitive —> "I can learn so much from others. There's always more to know."

Early on, they'll be fully immersed in their inner struggle, unaware of just how much it's holding them back. This will begin to change as their arc kicks into gear. Once they set out on their journey, your character will slowly discover the real truth of their story—though they'll resist this truth for as long as they can. It's this resistance that will cause conflict within your character, resulting in a difficult battle between the lessons they're learning and the harmful belief they can't seem to let go.

This internal fight is what will determine the arc your character follows, as well as the outcome of their transformation.

Characters who accept their truth and overcome their inner struggle will usually succeed, while those who reject their truth will fail. Because this truth is a key part of resolving your novel's core conflict, your character can't thrive without it. Only by making a choice they never could have made otherwise will they have what it takes to overcome the final challenge of their story.

Case Study: Katniss Everdeen

With those terms in mind, you might be wondering how they work in practice. This is where our case studies come in, which will appear repeatedly throughout this book, each focused on a particular aspect of your cast and character arcs. For this first case study, we'll be looking at Katniss Everdeen from *The Hunger Games*—specifically her inner struggle and truth.

If you're unfamiliar with this story, it takes place in a dystopian nation called Panem, where the powerful Capitol exploits and oppresses twelve surrounding districts. As punishment for a past rebellion, the Capitol hosts an annual "Hunger Games," where teenagers from each district are forced to fight to the death until only one winner remains.

Katniss' story begins on the eve of these games.

Katniss is the sole provider for her family, taking on that role after her father dies in a mining accident and her mother descends into despair. Though she's only sixteen, she's bitter and cynical, as well as fiercely protective. This protectiveness becomes important when her younger sister is chosen as a tribute for the games. Katniss knows that being chosen is as good as death, so she volunteers to take her sister's place. Though her chances of returning home are slim, her sister's life is more important than her own.

This triggers a long and difficult journey, where Katniss fights between a deep mistrust of others and the truth that there's more to living than basic survival:

- **Her Inner Struggle:** No one can be trusted—if she's going to survive, she has to do so alone.
- **Her Truth:** Survival isn't worth it if you abandon everything you value in the process.

How do these unfold?

Well, Katniss begins her arc fully consumed by her inner struggle. She's keenly aware of the Capitol's influence and thus holds everyone at arm's length. In her eyes, no one is safe, not even her closest allies.

Early on, this suspicious nature makes it hard for Katniss to find friends, accept advice, and stay alive in the hyper-competitive games. Fortunately, as she faces obstacles she can't handle alone, she's forced to realize her truth. Slowly—and with plenty of resistance—she welcomes allies into her circle, refuses to betray her values, and even risks her own safety to protect a girl who reminds her of her sister.

Still, Katniss knows she'll eventually have to kill any friends she makes to survive. The games can only have one winner, and so her inner struggle and truth continue fighting for dominance. This comes to a head during the finale of her story. With only her and a friend left in the arena, Katniss suggests they commit suicide rather than give the Capitol a winner. In doing so, she transforms as a character, embraces her truth, and lets go of the inner struggle that was holding her back—all while dealing a powerful blow to the Capitol!

This is the real victory of Katniss' story.

Though she started out isolated and angry because of her inner struggle, she ends her story a hero, returning home with a new belief that there's more to life than just survival. Her character arc is complete, and the internal conflict that was dragging her down has begun to heal.

Beyond an Inner Struggle

Understanding these two sides of your character's life is great, but there is one more question we need to address:

Where does their inner struggle come from?

You see, what makes Katniss' transformation work is that her inner struggle and truth feel like natural extensions of her character. Her suspicion of others is logical given her experiences, and her eventual truth aligns perfectly with her desire to protect and defend. These two elements, combined with things like her personality and mannerisms, create a character that feels believable and alive—and this should extend to your cast too.

Regardless of what your character's inner struggle and truth are, they need to feel like innate aspects of their personality, history, and worldview. Why does your character hold this harmful belief? What about this belief is so hard for them to let go? Most importantly, what triggers their inner struggle?

The answer comes down to two main things: their identity and their backstory.

Their Identity:

First up, your character's identity is how they perceive themselves and their role in the world around them. This could be connected to anything from their hobby or career, to their social status, nationality, family, or even physical traits. For instance, one character might identify as the class clown, while others see themselves as starving artists, beloved leaders, or social outcasts.

However, this is just one side of your character's identity. Alongside their beliefs about themselves, they'll also be affected by the beliefs of others—and this is where the two types of identity come into play:

- **Internal Identity:** Your character's perception of themselves and their place in their world. This is usually a result of their past experiences.
- **External Identity:** How others perceive your character based on their appearance, social status, or group affiliations. Typically, this will be out of your character's control.

These combine to determine both your character's perspective, as well as how they're treated by others. This is where identity becomes such a powerful tool for creating internal conflict. Whatever your character's identities are, they'll inform their beliefs, opportunities, and behavior, and thus the lessons they struggle to learn.

Their Backstory:

Alongside their identity, your characters will also have some sort of backstory. This is any key event or experience that defines who they are as a person, whether by shaping their identity or setting up important relationships.

Your character's backstory will also play a major role in triggering their inner struggle.

All of our beliefs come from somewhere, and that somewhere is often found in our history. Your character might have suffered from some long-term pain, such as growing up in a society that rejected them or living beneath a cruel regime. They could also have experienced some singular trauma in the form of a tragic event, loss, or fight. Either of these options can leave a major impact, eventually taking root as your character's inner struggle.

With that said, your character's backstory doesn't have to be tragic. Though the inner struggle is a harmful belief, that doesn't mean it's an intrinsically bad one—just that it's at odds with the lesson your character needs to learn.

In these cases, the origins of your character's inner struggle could be completely benign. For example, perhaps their older brother told them not to cry in public as a kid. Though their brother didn't mean anything harmful, their young mind ran with it, eventually morphing into the harmful belief that "they can never show weakness." While this seemingly small event might not look as important as an alien invasion or catastrophic flood, it can still fester over time into a deeply impactful moment of backstory.

Once you understand your character's harmful beliefs, figuring out their truth is fairly easy! This is the balm that will soothe their wounds. A character who believes they're worthless might learn that being different isn't shameful, just like a character who thinks they're better than others could find humility and patience. Whatever their truth is, this is the lesson they need to learn if they ever hope to overcome their inner struggle.

Of course, you're a writer—and that means you have a few extra things to consider when creating your cast:

- **Your Core Conflict:** Sometimes called your central conflict, this is the primary challenge, threat, or obstacle that defines the majority of your plot. Think of Frodo's quest to destroy the One Ring or Moana's fight to restore Te Fiti's heart.
- **Your Theme:** The "point" of your story. This is the connecting message that links your novel together, encompassing anything from specific lessons or morals to more general explorations of topics like power or love.

I've mentioned your core conflict a few times now, but only in passing. This is a critical component of your novel, not only because it drives your plot, but also because it's intrinsically tied to your characters. Your core conflict sets the stage for their character arcs by shaking up their normal life and pushing them to change. As this conflict comes onto the scene, they'll have to make the choice to engage with it, or risk suffering severe consequences. This is also closely linked to their inner struggle. Their inner struggle will act as an obstacle, preventing them from taking the steps needed to resolve this core conflict—at least until they overcome their harmful beliefs and change as a person.

As an example, consider a character like Luke Skywalker from *Star Wars: A New Hope*. The core conflict of that movie is the looming threat of the Death Star, a threat Luke eliminates when he successfully destroys it. However, this isn't an easy task, either physically or mentally. Alongside developing the practical skills needed to help the rebel cause, Luke also has to embrace his truth—that being faith in the Force. Without accepting this truth, Luke would have made the same mistakes as the other pilots and missed his only shot at victory.

Meanwhile, you'll also need to think about your theme.

Theme is an often nebulous topic, one a lot of writers shy away from. However, theme is actually fairly straightforward, at least in this context. Your theme is the "point" of your story, acting as the connective tissue that binds your novel together. This could be anything from a specific message like "love conquers fear," to a more general exploration of topics like "the meaning of justice."

Whatever your theme is, you'll want to keep it in mind when crafting your character's internal conflicts. Returning to Luke, his story focuses on a theme of faith. He's a simple farm boy, meaning it's easy to understand why he struggles to accept his place in his larger world. This contrasts with his truth of faith in the Force. By trusting in this larger power, he discovers a strength in himself that reshapes his views of his own potential.

This extends to the rest of the cast too.

We'll be returning to *A New Hope* later in this book, but for now, "faith" is a recurring issue throughout this movie. Han Solo struggles to have faith in the rebel effort, while characters like Obi-Wan Kenobi and Princess Leia encourage both Luke and Han to believe in the Force. Through this, the theme of faith slowly winds through every aspect of the story, binding its cast together into a cohesive whole.

When combined with your novel's core conflict and the other pieces we've discussed, this will go a long way towards making your characters' journeys feel complete.

Lessons from Chapter Two

Ultimately, this chapter was a sampler of some pretty important topics. Inner struggle, truth, identity, and backstory will come up a lot throughout this book, so I hope you'll keep this chapter in mind as we move forward.

As one final refresher, here are the six things that will define your characters' arcs:

- **Their Inner Struggle:** A harmful belief that holds your character back throughout your story. Sometimes called their lie or wound, this belief prevents them from achieving their goals and resolving the core conflict of your novel.
- **Their Truth:** The lesson your character needs to learn in order to overcome their inner struggle. This stands in direct contrast to their harmful beliefs, making this truth the "message" of their story. Accepting their truth is the final test of their arc.
- **Their Identity:** How your character perceives themselves and their place in the world around them, as well as how other characters perceive them.

- **Their Backstory:** The one or two experiences that define your character's life. These events are usually the source of their inner struggle and identity.
- **Your Core Conflict:** Sometimes called your central conflict, this is the primary challenge, threat, or obstacle that defines the majority of your plot. Think of Frodo's quest to destroy the One Ring or Moana's fight to restore Te Fiti's heart.
- **Your Theme:** The "point" of your story. This is the connecting message that links your novel together, encompassing anything from specific lessons or morals to more general explorations of topics like power or love.

With that said, there is one piece of this puzzle we haven't touched on yet—and that is motivation.

While your character's inner struggle, truth, identity, and backstory will go a long way towards pushing them to grow and evolve, they need some goal to spur them to action in the first place. This "story goal" will be our focus for the next chapter, before we wrap up the basics and turn our attention to your characters' arcs in Part Two!

In the meantime, here are a few questions to help you apply what you've learned to your cast:

- What harmful belief is holding your character back at the start of their story?
- What lesson will they need to learn in order to overcome that belief?
- How do their identity and backstory lay the groundwork for their inner struggle?

- How will your core conflict force their life to change?

Once you've answered these questions, I'll see you in Chapter Three!

3

THE IMPORTANCE OF MOTIVATION

If you want to write engaging characters, you need to ask yourself a few questions:

- Why does your character begin their journey?
- What lights a fire under their feet, pushing them forward against impossible odds?
- What makes the trials ahead worth the effort?

Over the years, I've found many writers overlook these questions when planning their cast. All too often, we get so caught up in exploring our plot and setting up exciting conflicts that we forget that our characters need a reason to take action too—beyond just "that's how the story goes." Though it's easy to forget, your plot won't be meaningful to your characters by default. Even the most proactive among them will still need some force pushing them into the fray.

So, what is this force, and how can you find it for your cast?

Well, the answer is motivation—specifically your character's story goal!

Exploring the Story Goal

Motivation is a critical part of writing memorable characters, because motivation is what gives their journey meaning.

Think about it—if you're running to the grocery store to grab some milk, that's not a particularly interesting story. However, if you need that milk because you just ate a Carolina Reaper, suddenly the whole affair has a bit more urgency. You have a clear, strong motivation to get to the store as quickly as possible, giving an otherwise unremarkable grocery run a whole new layer of impact.

This extends to your characters too.

Motivation is the driving force that will not only push them to face conflicts and challenges, but also learn and grow. When things get hard, this motivation is what will keep them from giving up. It'll also tell readers a lot about who your character is as a person. A character that's motivated by greed or selfishness will be very different than one motivated by altruism or generosity. Though readers cheer for Robin Hood, most would condemn your average bank robber.

Of course, lots of things will motivate your cast throughout your novel. Hunger, cold, loneliness, and fear are all important forces that will encourage your characters to take action. However, these smaller motivations are mostly reactionary. Your character steps into the hot summer sun and ducks away to find shade. Their stomach rumbles, so they head off to prepare lunch. This creates a nice chain of cause and effect, but it doesn't create the kind of forward momentum your character needs to carry them through your story.

Instead, this is the job of their story goal.

Your character's story goal is the primary motivation or desire that drives their actions throughout your novel—above and beyond the smaller forces I just described. Often, your characters will already have this goal in mind when your novel begins, though some will only find it after your core conflict crashes onto the scene. Either way, this shapes their journey in two key ways:

- **Triggering Their Arc:** Your character's story goal is what will force them to engage with your novel's conflict. Not only will this drag them (often kicking and screaming) into your plot, but it'll also jumpstart their character arc.
- **Connecting With Readers:** Your character's story goal should also reveal a lot about who they are as a person. This provides valuable context for your readers, allowing them to identify with your character and root for them as their story unfolds.

Typically, your character's story goal will remain static for the majority of your novel, though it is possible for their goal to evolve as their journey unfolds. Most characters start their story with a single goal that lasts from beginning to end, but others shift their focus towards a new goal halfway through their arc. Some might even struggle between multiple, conflicting story goals, only settling on one or the other after much inner turmoil.

You can see this at work in a few popular stories:

- ***Star Wars: A New Hope* (1977):** Luke is motivated by a desire to defeat the Empire and avenge his family. Luke has one story goal from beginning to end.
- ***How to Train Your Dragon* (2010):** Hiccup is

motivated by a desire to be accepted as a Viking, and later to be accepted as himself. Hiccup gives up his old story goal for a new goal as he grows.
- ***Casablanca* (1942):** Rick is motivated by two conflicting desires: to protect his own interests and to help Ilsa escape the Nazis. Rick struggles between two goals until the end of his story.

What this all comes down to is stakes.

Stakes are the consequences your characters will face if they fail to achieve their story goals, and they're why these central motivations matter. When the consequences of failure are clear, there's suddenly a sense of urgency, until even the most intimidating obstacles aren't enough to turn your character away. These stakes also ensnare your readers. As your plot unfolds, readers will want to stick around, because they know your characters have something to lose.

Fortunately, this doesn't mean every novel you write needs some world-ending threat. While alien invasions and deadly attacks create obvious motivations, losing a spelling bee or failing a test can be just as impactful—it simply depends on your story!

Instead, the most important thing is that the stakes of failure are personally relevant to your characters. This heightens the tension and forces your cast to take all kinds of risks, thus encouraging them to grow and change.

For instance, in *A New Hope,* the Empire is a threat to the galaxy—but even more than that, they're a threat to the people Luke loves. Meanwhile, Hiccup's stakes are being shunned by his community and eventually losing his new friend, while Rick's stakes are being forced to either give up his business or betray the love of his life. These various stakes are what make these characters' story goals meaningful. If they fail to achieve their goals, they each stand to lose something they deeply care about.

What Motivates Your Character?

Figuring out your character's story goal works much like choosing their inner struggle and truth from the previous chapter. This is all about deciding what feels right for them as a person, as well as what your story needs to thrive:

Who They Are:

Your character's story goal should feel like a natural result of who they are as a person. This is shaped by their identity, backstory, and inner struggle from Chapter Two, along with things like their personality, hopes, and fears.

Usually, this goal is your character's attempt to "solve" their inner struggle, even if that attempt is misguided. You know that their truth is the real secret to healing their wounds, but they won't figure that out for some time. Instead, their inner struggle will form the backdrop for all of their desires, their story goal included.

To help with this, consider these questions:

- What does your character fear most?
- What would they do to avoid this fear?
- How do they perceive themselves?
- How do others perceive them?
- Do they want to change or maintain these identities?
- Are they seeking answers, and if so, what for?

- What do they feel they're responsible for?
- What do they want to change about their world?
- What cause are they fighting for?
- Do they have a dream they want to achieve?

The Role They Play:

Alongside things like their inner struggle and identity, your character's story goal should also mesh with the needs of your novel.

This is closely tied to your novel's core conflict—specifically how your character's story goal gets them involved in that conflict. For instance, a character like Disney's Rapunzel is motivated to see the floating lights that appear on her birthday, forcing her to accept a stranger's help and go against her mother's wishes. Meanwhile, Katniss Everdeen from our case study in Chapter Two is focused on survival. If she had her way, she would ignore every aspect of the games; but, in order to achieve her story goal, she has to play along.

To help with this, consider these questions:

- What is your novel's core conflict?
- How will your character's story goal force them to engage with that conflict?
- Does their story goal put them at odds with other members of your cast?
- What will this goal push them to do that they wouldn't do otherwise?

No matter what your character's story goal ends up being, it needs to be specific and measurable.

A great example of this is the difference between "getting better at soccer" and "becoming team captain before the season ends." Both of these goals could count as story goals, but only the second one is a *good* story goal. It has a concrete end point, defined by a specific status and a specific time frame. In contrast, the first is much more vague. Getting "better" at something is highly subjective, meaning it lacks the kind of tension and forward momentum a well-chosen story goal should provide.

Alongside being specific, good story goals also:

- **Create Conflict:** The best story goals put your character at odds with others in your novel. This sparks conflict and disagreement, even between friends and allies. By giving your characters conflicting story goals, you ensure there are plenty of interesting obstacles between them and what they want to achieve.
- **Appear Early On:** Your character's story goal will drive all of their actions—meaning you need to introduce it early. While some characters won't realize their story goal until your plot shakes up their life, you want to establish their goal as soon as you reasonably can.
- **Strike Deep:** Finally, the best story goals are deeply personal to your character. Whatever motivates them, it should tie directly into their core identities, traits, and beliefs.

So long as your character's story goal meets these requirements, you should be good to go!

The Goals of Heroes and Villains

Above and beyond the rest of your cast, there are two characters whose motivation warrants a bit of extra attention:

- **Your Protagonist:** This is your novel's central character, as well as your story's focal point. They'll be the primary catalyst of change for your plot, making them one of the most important characters in your novel.
- **Your Antagonist:** In contrast, the antagonist directly opposes your protagonist. They're the main destructive force in your novel, fanning the flames of your core conflict and acting as the final obstacle of your protagonist's quest.

Why do these two characters matter so much?

Well, not only are they vital to your story, but their story goals also play a major role in shaping your novel—above and beyond the rest of your cast. Your protagonist's story goal will form the backbone of your plot, while your antagonist's story goal will create hurdles that hinder their progress. Both of these characters are intrinsically tied to your novel's core conflict, meaning you need to keep that conflict in mind when choosing their story goals.

For your antagonist specifically, simply obstructing your protagonist isn't enough here.

Far too many writers forget their villains are characters too, and that they'll have their own desires, motivations, fears, and personality. Because of this, your antagonist's story goal should be a reflection of who they are, rather than just a way to hurt your hero. For example, Sauron's story goal in *The*

Lord of the Rings is to reunite with the One Ring and regain his full power, while Darth Vader in *Star Wars* is focused on destroying the rebel cause in order to please his master. Though these goals absolutely cause problems for their heroes, they also go beyond simply hurting Frodo or Luke.

Whatever your antagonist's story goal is, just remember that it should feel like a natural part of who they are, the same as any other character.

Lessons from Chapter Three

Ultimately, a clear story goal is the glue that will bind your characters together.

Combine this goal with the elements we discussed in the previous chapter, and suddenly you have a solid foundation from which to build vibrant characters. You know the beliefs that will hold your character back, the identities and experiences that inform who they are, and the lesson they'll eventually need to learn if they want to succeed. With their story goal now in hand, you also have the spark that will trigger their journey. This motivation is what will drive them throughout every stage of their arc, growing and evolving until it eventually changes their life in unexpected (and long-lasting) ways.

With that foundation set, it's time to dig into arcs themselves.

Though we're far from finished with this book, everything we'll discuss from here on out will build on what you've just learned. For those of you who were already familiar with character development, this hopefully served as a helpful refresher—or, if you're totally new here, a quick crash course! Starting in the next chapter, we'll begin unpacking all the ways your characters' unique arcs might unfold.

In the meantime, here are a few questions to help you apply what you've learned to your cast:

- What is your character's primary motivation throughout their story?
- Does this motivation change over time?
- Will they have to struggle between multiple conflicting story goals?
- How does this story goal get them involved in your novel's core conflict?

Once you've answered these questions, I'll see you in Part Two!

II

UNDERSTANDING CHARACTER ARCS

"There are only two or three human stories, and they go on repeating themselves as fiercely as if they had never happened before."

WILLA CATHER, AMERICAN WRITER AND JOURNALIST

4

THE TWO TYPES OF CHARACTER ARCS

Most stories can be boiled down to a pretty simple formula:

> *"Someone wants something, faces obstacles in pursuit of that goal, learns an important lesson, and changes as a person."*

At first glance, this does a decent job of covering the bases. We have a character, some sort of conflict, a clear motivation, and a final outcome, along with subtle hints of an inner struggle and truth appearing along the way. These bases have been our focus so far, and they'll go a long way towards helping you write engaging characters.

However, on their own, they aren't enough.

While this basic journey makes sense, it's actually hiding a whole variety of unique story beats, turning points, catalysts, and options, all tucked just out of sight. These are the pieces that will take your cast from "meh" to "beloved," because this is where character arcs really come into focus. After all, those useful frameworks we touched on back in Chapter One aren't just built on inner conflict and motivation—they need some kind of structure too.

So, as we begin Part Two, it's time to shift our attention away from the basics, and towards the (much wider) world of character arcs themselves!

Primary vs. Secondary Arcs

As you might remember from back in Chapter One, character arcs are frameworks based on universal patterns that help writers create dynamic characters. These are characters that evolve and change throughout their adventures, and (more importantly) change in ways that feel natural.

This makes character arcs a fantastic tool, not only for understanding your cast, but also for writing characters your readers can relate to. Everyone experiences periods of transition in their lives. The better we can capture those feelings of uncertainty on the page, the more our readers will get invested in our characters' stories.

Of course, until now, we've been describing these arcs as something of a monolith. However, the truth is that there's more to character arcs than meets the eye! Far from being a standardized journey from start to finish, character arcs come in two main forms:

- **Primary Character Arcs:** These arcs determine the overarching inner journey your character goes on, as well as the final outcome of their story. Your character's primary arc can be either positive, negative, or flat.

- **Secondary Character Arcs:** These arcs focus on specific story beats and patterns that help your characters fulfill specialized roles such as coming of age, the chosen one, or redemption. Secondary arcs are optional.

Between these two types of arcs, primary arcs are the big-picture journeys of change that most writers think of when discussing character arcs. Your characters might grow and embrace their truth, or perhaps succumb to their inner struggle. Alternatively, if they already know their truth, their story will be about teaching that truth to others, while facing resistance and obstacles along the way.

PRIMARY VS. SECONDARY ARCS

Primary

These arcs determine the overarching inner journey of your character, as well as the final outcome of their story.

- *The Positive Arc*
- *The Negative Arc*
- *The Flat Arc*

Secondary

These arcs focus on specific story beats and patterns that help your characters fulfill more specialized roles.

- *The Hero's Arc*
- *The Lover's Arc*
- *The Redemption Arc*

In contrast, secondary arcs are much more specialized.

These arcs focus on common patterns of change found in different types of characters, such as the hero, hermit, or chosen one. These journeys come up in storytelling again and again, but they aren't tropes. Instead, these are experiences all of us can relate to, such as growing up, accepting responsibility, or loving another person. This is what makes secondary arcs "universal." Unlike genre-specific tropes like the knight in shining armor or the damsel in distress from fairytales, secondary arcs provide a blueprint for writing about specific, shared stories.

With that said, not every character needs a secondary arc—and this is where character arcs start to form layers.

Primary arcs act as your character's foundation, while secondary arcs fill in the details. All characters (at least those with their own arcs) will have some form of primary arc. Meanwhile, secondary arcs are optional. Some characters will do just fine with a standalone primary arc, while others might benefit from the structure provided by a secondary arc. If they do have an additional secondary arc, these two will combine together, forming a unique pair that shapes every beat of that character's story.

This adds a whole new level to your cast, opening up tons of fascinating options—from the flat hero's arc to the negative rogue's arc. In total, there are nearly seventy-two different combinations to choose from, each with their own quirks and uses!

An Eight-Part Structure

On the surface, this amount of variety is probably a bit intimidating. Seventy-two options is nothing to sneeze at, and figuring out how to combine these types of arcs might not feel intuitive at first glance.

Luckily, even with this variety, primary and secondary arcs are still arcs, meaning they both follow the same basic rules. Regardless of the type of arc you're dealing with, it'll still act as a framework for writing cathartic stories, creating believable change, and ensuring your story flows smoothly.

Because of this, all character arcs follow a similar eight-part structure.

The Beginning:

Your character begins in their "normal world." Here they're suffering from some inner struggle, which is preventing them from achieving their goals and finding happiness—though they don't recognize this harmful belief just yet.

This starting point is how readers will judge your character's growth as your story unfolds.

Catalyst:

Next, some catalyst will come along that forces your character to make a choice. Whatever they decide to do, this is their first point of no return, dragging them into the conflict of your story and thus kicking their arc into motion. Usually, this is where you'll introduce their story goal.

The Reactive Phase:

With your character's life turned upside down, it's time for them to flounder. Here they'll struggle to get their bearings, learn and adapt, and hopefully come to terms with their new situation.

For the most part, this means your character is stuck reacting to external events, even as they try to pursue their story goal. Their inner struggle is still in full force, but their truth is slowly coming into view.

Turning Point:

This comes to a head at your character's next crossroad, about halfway through their arc. They've begun to understand their truth, meaning now it's time to prove themselves through a major test.

Typically, your character will overcome this test and be rewarded with new allies, knowledge, or skills. However, they haven't conquered their inner struggle just yet. While they think they've solved their problems, this is a false victory, one that will come back to haunt them later on.

The Active Phase:

From there we enter the Active Phase. Your character finally has the confidence and resources needed to pursue their story goal full force, rather than simply responding to outside forces. They believe they've embraced their truth, but their inner struggle is quietly holding them back. Though they think they've solved their problems (or at least have a plan to do so), they don't realize that they're marching towards failure.

Regression:

This failure comes in the form of the Regression, the third crossroad of your character's arc. Here they'll face a painful defeat, one that's a direct result of their inner struggle. The solution they thought they had found will prove false, and they'll be forced to stop and reflect on both their journey so far and their next steps.

Choice:

From there, the Choice is where your character will prove their transformation through action. To do so, they'll have to make a difficult choice, one they couldn't have made without the journey they just went on. If all goes well, your character will accept their truth and triumph—but it's also possible they learned the wrong lessons. If that happens, their inner struggle will slowly consume them, and the consequences will be severe.

The End:

Finally, we reach your character's resolution, where readers will see the result of their arc. This ending should strike a sharp contrast with where your character began. The more significant their transformation is, the more different their ending will be compared to their starting point.

This structure is based on common patterns of change found in nearly all stories. The beginning and end are the two contrasting points that highlight your character's transformation, while the phases in between ensure that transformation unfolds organically over time.

Meanwhile, your character will make a variety of important decisions at key crossroads like the Catalyst, Turning Point, Regression, and Choice. These give them a chance to prove they're growing, shaping both your plot and their arc in one fell swoop.

Lessons from Chapter Four

Character arcs are a fantastic tool for building memorable casts, precisely because of how much variety they offer. With dozens of combinations to choose from, you'll have plenty of unique story beats to fuel your own stories, offer inspiration, and troubleshoot difficult characters.

Even better, you don't have to memorize every possible arc!

Because your cast will be built on a combination of both primary and secondary arcs, you'll only need a handful of building blocks in order to craft a nearly infinite variety of characters. So, if these options seem intimidating now, don't worry. Between the eight-part structure we explored in this chapter and the tips and advice to come, I'll be here to guide you every step of the way.

In the meantime, here are a few questions to help you apply what you've learned to your cast:

- What key turning points do you already have in mind for your character, if any?
- What major event could trigger their arc?
- How will your plot test and challenge them as their story unfolds?
- What choice will they eventually make to prove they've changed as a person?

Once you've answered these questions, I'll see you in Chapter Five!

5

POSITIVE, NEGATIVE, AND FLAT

Three transformations stand at the core of character arcs: heroes, villains, and teachers.

Often, arcs are discussed as being a character's journey from flawed to not flawed, and in some cases that's true. However, this ignores the bigger picture. Not every arc ends on a happy note, and some aren't even about your character in the first place. Just like your cast might be full of people who grow and thrive, it could also feature characters who fail, decay, support, or uplift, blending together into a complex picture not unlike our real world.

This is where character arcs start coming into focus—specifically in the form of primary arcs.

The Three Primary Arcs

As you'll hopefully remember from the previous chapter, primary arcs are all about building your character's foundation. These are the arcs that determine their overarching internal change, shaping not only the outcome of their story, but also the choices they make along the way.

In total, there are three primary arcs:

- **The Positive Arc:** The positive arc is all about growth. Here your character starts out suffering from some inner struggle, faces tests and trials, and ultimately realizes an important truth. It's through this truth that they overcome their inner struggle and resolve the conflict of their story.
- **The Negative Arc:** In contrast, the negative arc focuses on decay. Here your character also starts out suffering from some inner struggle, but rather than overcome it, they succumb to it. They refuse to embrace their truth and thus devolve into a worse version of themselves, leaving them unable to resolve the conflict of their story.
- **The Flat Arc:** Finally, flat arc characters already know their truth when their story begins. Instead, rather than struggling to grow as a person, their arc is about sharing their truth with those who need it—even in the face of great difficulty.

Right away, you'll probably notice that one of these arcs isn't quite like its peers. The flat arc is something of a "black sheep" in the world of character development, at least when compared to the other two primary arcs. While the positive and negative arcs center on your character's own internal change, the flat arc is all about how they change other people. This shifts the focus of your story away from your character and towards the world around them.

Of course, positive and negative arc characters will still affect their outside world—while flat arc characters will still struggle and deal with change. The difference is simply the focus of these arcs. Positive and negative arcs are all about your character's personal journey, while flat arcs are more interested in how they affect others.

THE THREE PRIMARY ARCS

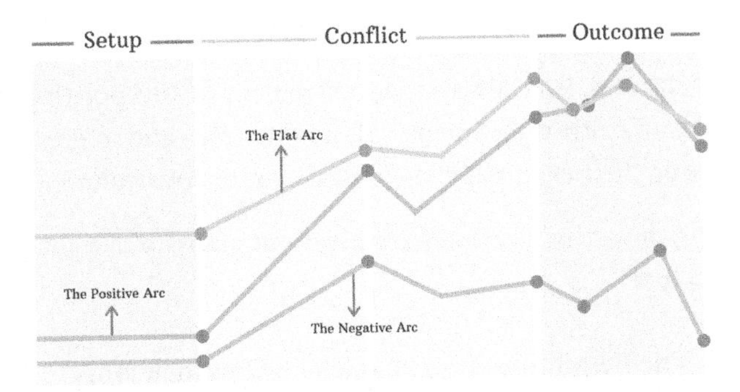

Let's explore each of these arcs in a bit more detail.

The Positive Arc:

The first of the two change arcs, the positive character arc is all about growth.

In a positive arc, your character will face a series of tests and trials that force them to reassess their behavior and beliefs. As they do so, they'll slowly realize an important truth. Though they'll resist this truth at first, they'll eventually learn to embrace it, using it to overcome their inner struggle and triumph over the conflict of their story.

This makes positive arcs some of the most common character arcs in fiction. They're uplifting and energizing, and they leave readers feeling good about the transformation they just witnessed. You can see this at work in characters such as Katniss Everdeen, Johnny Castle from *Dirty Dancing*, Katara from *Avatar: The Last Airbender*, or even Thor from the Marvel Cinematic Universe, among thousands of others.

Basically, the positive arc is a journey of success—though that success isn't always guaranteed. Even the positive arc will suffer from moments of doubt, fear, and regression, making their eventual victory all the more powerful.

Here's how this character arc plays out across our eight-part structure:

- **The Beginning:** Your character begins their story suffering from some inner struggle, leaving them unsatisfied if not outright unhappy. Despite this, they aren't aware of their inner struggle just yet. Though they may have a goal they think will fix their problems, their true arc hasn't begun.
- **Catalyst:** This starts to change when some disruptive force crashes onto the scene. Whatever this is, it causes your character to make a choice that embroils them in the conflict of your story.
- **The Reactive Phase:** From there, we enter the Reactive Phase, where your character will have to adjust to their new situation. Here they'll learn important lessons, face tests and trials, and slowly get their bearings. Along the way, their inner struggle will get them into trouble, and their truth will come into view—though they won't accept it just yet.
- **Turning Point:** Next, the positive arc character will

face a major challenge, giving them a chance to prove just how much they've learned. In order to overcome this test, they'll have to embrace their truth for the first time, and will ultimately be rewarded with the allies, knowledge, or tools they need to start taking charge of their journey.

- **The Active Phase:** After the Turning Point, your character has a new plan to resolve your core conflict. However, they still haven't dealt with their inner struggle—even if they think they have. Though they've begun to embrace their truth, their inner struggle is still holding them back.
- **Regression:** This leads to a major defeat. Your character's plans will fail, and they'll be forced to reassess everything they believe. This is their chance to finally confront their inner struggle openly, accept their truth, and let go of the harmful beliefs obstructing their growth.
- **Choice:** Luckily, the positive arc character survives the Regression—meaning now they must prove their transformation through action. Here they'll make some decision they never could have made without accepting their truth, allowing them to triumph over the conflict of their story.
- **The End:** Finally, the positive arc comes full circle, showing how your character's life has changed for the better as a result of their journey!

This positive character arc is often treated as the "default arc"—even within this book.

Not only is this arc by far the most common, but it also acts as a great baseline for understanding the many journeys your characters could go on. Within the positive arc, your character starts out flawed and suffering from a deep inner struggle, before learning an important lesson that allows them to overcome that struggle. This is an impactful journey, one that can apply to a wide range of stories and thus act as a solid foundation for more complex characters.

The Negative Arc:

Of course, not all journeys have a happy ending...

Much like the positive arc, the negative arc is all about change—however, not the good kind of change. This arc follows a character as they slowly wither, overwhelmed by their inner struggle and unable to correct course. This downfall can happen in any number of ways, from a simple refusal to accept their truth, to an active desire to destroy their enemies. Think of characters like Anakin Skywalker from *Star Wars*, Jay Gatsby from *The Great Gatsby*, or Lord Macbeth from Shakespeare's *Macbeth*. Though these characters start their stories much like any other, they end them as a hollow shell, all because their inner struggles were too great to overcome.

This is what makes negative arcs particularly interesting. At its start, it doesn't look that different from the positive arc. Both are primary arcs, meaning both follow a similar setup:

- **The Beginning:** Your character begins their story suffering from some inner struggle, leaving them unsatisfied if not outright unhappy. Despite this, they aren't aware of their inner struggle just yet. Though they may have a goal they think will fix their problems, their true arc hasn't begun.
- **Catalyst:** This starts to change when some disruptive force crashes onto the scene. Whatever this is, it

causes your character to make a choice that embroils them in the conflict of your story.

- **The Reactive Phase:** From there, we enter the Reactive Phase, where your character will have to adjust to their new situation. Here they'll learn important lessons, face tests and trials, and slowly get their bearings. Along the way, their inner struggle will get them into trouble, and their truth will come into view—though they won't accept it just yet.
- **Turning Point:** Next, the negative arc character will face a major challenge, giving them a chance to prove just how much they've learned. However, unlike the positive arc character, the negative arc character has learned the wrong lessons. Though they overcome this test, doing so reinforces their inner struggle, setting them up for failure down the road.
- **The Active Phase:** After the Turning Point, your character has a new plan to resolve the conflict of your story. This is where their inner struggle begins to take on a life of its own. Though your character might seem in control, they're slowly unraveling beneath the surface, making increasingly destructive choices as their inner struggle grows.
- **Regression:** This leads to a major defeat. Your character's plans will fail, and they'll be forced to reassess everything they believe. Unfortunately, the negative arc character is unable to give up their inner struggle, instead rejecting their truth. After this point, there's no going back—they're too invested to turn around now.
- **Choice:** This spirals into the Choice, where your character will face one final test. Here they'll double down on their inner struggle, committing some harmful act that proves just how much they've fallen.

  This leaves the conflict of their story unresolved, or resolved with horrible consequences.
- **The End:** Finally, the negative arc comes full circle, showing the consequences of your character's decay. Because of their actions, they'll lose something meaningful, be that their life, loved ones, soul, or status.

Overall, the first half of this negative arc isn't too remarkable. Just like the positive arc, the negative arc character begins suffering from some inner struggle, makes the choice to engage with their story's conflict, and eventually faces a turning point that appears to solve their problems.

Unfortunately, this is where things start to unravel. Whereas the positive arc character uses their truth to solve their Turning Point, the negative arc character clings to their inner struggle. Rather than question their harmful beliefs, they embrace them, and for every setback they face, they dig their heels in further. Even if they recognize they're on the wrong path, they simply don't have the strength or support needed to break this cycle. As the second half of their arc unfolds, they transform into a worse version of themselves, eventually becoming a mirror image of their positive arc brethren.

This downfall can happen in a variety of ways.

Many negative arc characters actively embrace their darker side, so caught up in their inner struggle that doing so seems like the best choice. Others might have the right intentions, but are led astray, usually by other characters. And finally, some negative arc characters simply get trapped in a cycle of destruction they don't know how to escape from—even though they know their choices are wrong.

Either way, the important thing is that the negative arc character *chooses* their path. Even if their choices are swayed by others or forced by circumstances outside of their control, it'll still be their decisions that drag them down. This ensures their decay feels like a genuine transformation, one directly linked to their inner struggle and thus a product of their own personal flaws.

The Flat Arc:

Finally, we come to the flat arc.

While the two primary arcs we've discussed so far have been about change, the flat arc is a bit different. Rather than focusing on a character as they transform their life and confront their own inner demons, the flat arc is about healing the inner struggles of other people. Because of this, the flat arc character begins their story already knowing their truth, while the world around them rejects it.

You can see this arc at work in characters like Mattie Ross from *True Grit* or Steve Rogers from *Captain America*. Both of these characters have incredibly strong convictions, and those convictions end up being right. As their stories unfold, their journeys are less about growing within themselves, and more about guiding the people around them as they fight to teach their community.

All of this makes the flat arc a fascinating journey, and definitely the odd man out among the primary arcs we've studied. Fortunately, this arc still follows the same eight part structure—though with a few minor twists:

- **The Beginning:** Your character begins their story already knowing an important truth, while the world around them rejects that truth. Their community is suffering from a powerful inner struggle, one that leaves both your character and the people around them unhappy, vulnerable, and unsatisfied.

- **Catalyst:** This starts to change when some disruptive force crashes onto the scene. Whatever this is, it causes your character to make a choice that embroils them in the conflict of your story.
- **The Reactive Phase:** From there, we enter the Reactive Phase, where your character will have to adjust to their new situation. Here they'll learn important lessons, face tests and trials, and slowly find their bearings. Along the way, they'll have to confront their world's inner struggle, and their own truth will be tested.
- **Turning Point:** Next, the flat arc character will face a major challenge, giving them a chance to prove their truth is right. In order to overcome this test, they'll have to stay true to themselves, and will ultimately be rewarded with the allies, knowledge, or tools they need to start taking charge of their journey.
- **The Active Phase:** After the Turning Point, your character has a new plan to resolve your core conflict. However, their world hasn't overcome its inner struggle just yet—though they've likely convinced a few people to join their side. This inner struggle is still causing trouble, and that trouble is beginning to escalate.
- **Regression:** This leads to a major defeat. Your character's plans will fail, and they'll be forced to reassess everything they believe. This is a moment of temptation, when your character's truth will be called into question. If they're to succeed, they must hold on to that truth, even if they understand it in a new light in the process.

- **Choice:** Luckily, the flat arc character survives the Regression—meaning now they must face their community's inner struggle head on. Here they'll make some decision no one else could, putting their truth into action and thus triumphing over the conflict of your story.
- **The End:** Finally, the flat arc comes to an end, showing how your character's truth has changed the world around them for the better.

The final stages of this arc are yet one more place where the flat arc diverges from the other two primary arcs. While the positive and negative arc focus on how your character's life has been transformed, the flat arc is more concerned with your character's community.

How has their truth healed the world around them? How will their lessons affect life going forward?

Of course, since the flat arc isn't focused on your character's personal growth, you might be wondering—what about their own transformation?

Change is a vital ingredient for creating catharsis, and thus a major part of writing engaging character arcs. Fortunately, the flat arc does feature plenty of change, just with a more external focus. Flat arc characters often struggle with feelings of doubt and uncertainty, especially when their truth is challenged. They might be ostracized or dismissed for what they believe, or simply brushed off. Because of this, most flat arc characters start their story hiding their truth from others, only revealing it as their journey unfolds. While they already know the important lesson of their journey, having the strength to share that lesson won't always be easy.

Flat arc characters also make plenty of mistakes, and thus run into conflict!

Perhaps they're too heavy-handed, causing others to balk at the lessons they're trying to share. Or, maybe they catch themselves giving in to their world's inner struggle. All of these hurdles will get the flat arc character into trouble, and all of them are things they'll need to learn from as your novel wears on.

Though it might not seem like it on the surface, a well-written flat arc includes just as much conflict and change as any other, even if your character knows their truth from the beginning.

With these primary arcs in mind, you should be able to see that the positive and negative arc form something of a mirror image. At the start, they look almost identical—but, while the positive arc character learns the *right* lessons, the negative arc character learns the *wrong* ones.

Meanwhile, the flat arc is off doing its own thing.

While the positive and negative arc characters are struggling within themselves, the flat arc character is struggling against their world. Because of this, they never discover some big truth that solves their problems. Instead, they've known their truth all along, and now need to prove that truth to the people around them.

This leaves you with three types of primary arcs, as well as three corresponding stories:

- The Positive Arc — Growth and Learning

- The Negative Arc — Destruction and Decay
- The Flat Arc — Guidance and Healing

Case Study: Elle Woods, Michael Corleone, and Princess Nausicaä

We can discuss these primary arcs for days, but honestly, nothing replaces seeing them at work in an actual character. Usually, our case studies won't focus on so many stories at once—but, in this instance, it should be worth the extra time.

So, let's take a brief tour through three fascinating films:

- *Legally Blonde* (2001)
- *The Godfather* (1972)
- *Nausicaä of the Valley of the Wind* (1984)

Elle Woods — The Positive Arc:

If you've never watched *Legally Blonde*, it's a lighthearted, bubbly comedy about a young woman named Elle Woods.

Elle is obsessed with fashion and is your stereotypical "ditzy SoCal blonde"—except, she isn't. Elle is actually extremely intelligent, but the people around her rarely look past her appearance. Because of this, Elle starts her story deeply concerned with how other people see her. To her, her self-worth is defined by others' opinions, especially the opinions of her boyfriend Warner *(The Beginning)*.

This begins to change after Warner dumps her.

Warner has been accepted to Harvard Law, and doesn't think Elle is "serious enough" to toe the line among future senators and judges. Desperate to win him back, Elle decides she'll apply to Harvard Law too. After six long months of studying, she's granted admission *(Catalyst).*

However, Warner doesn't react the way she expects. Once Elle arrives at Harvard, she finds Warner engaged to another law student named Vivian and loathe to talk to her. Meanwhile, her fellow students treat her with contempt because of her looks *(The Reactive Phase).* All of this culminates in Elle confronting Warner after being humiliated by Vivian, where she realizes he'll never respect her—no matter how much she achieves.

This is the first time Elle embraces her truth. Rather than give up, she decides she'll become a successful lawyer on her own *(Turning Point)*!

Armed with renewed confidence, Elle thrives at law school and is soon accepted into a prestigious internship with Professor Callahan, where she's tasked with defending a woman accused of murder. Slowly but surely, she earns the trust of her client and unravels the case *(The Active Phase).* Her goal appears in sight, at least until Callahan reveals his true colors. Luring Elle into a room alone, he propositions her for sex, crushing her confidence and making her feel like she's back to square one *(Regression).*

Fortunately, this is a positive arc, meaning this Regression isn't the end of Elle's story.

Thanks to the support of her friends, Elle returns to defend her case, ousting Callahan and ultimately proving her client's innocence *(Choice).* In doing so, Elle shows herself to be a capable lawyer. She graduates from law school with honors, surrounded by friends and allies who truly support her. Best of all, Elle no longer doubts her self-worth *(The End).* Rather than look to others to confirm her value, she's secure in the knowledge that she's worthy of respect—thus completing her positive character arc!

Michael Corleone — The Negative Arc:

Compared to Elle, Michael Corleone follows a different path.

The protagonist of *The Godfather,* Michael starts out as the youngest son of Vito Corleone, the Don of New York City's powerful Corleone crime family. Michael, however, is not particularly interested in his father's business. He was a Marine in World War II, and is now settling into life back home with his girlfriend Kay. Though he's deeply loyal to his family, he intends to live within the law *(The Beginning).*

Unfortunately for Michael, life has other plans for him.

After Vito rejects the advances of a rival family, they attempt to assassinate him, shooting him while he's out buying oranges. Panicked, Michael races to be with his family *(Catalyst).* Initially, he does his best to stay above the fray, but this falls to the wayside after a second attempt on his father's life *(The Reactive Phase).* Enraged by what's happening to the people he loves, Michael volunteers to murder the men who attacked Vito. After killing them both, he's sent into hiding for his protection *(Turning Point).*

This begins Michael's downfall. Now a part of his family's war, Michael is a target for everything from car bombings to assassinations—and, though he survives, things back home grow worse. Bitter and jaded, he returns to take the reins of the Corleone crime family, reuniting with Kay as a changed man. Though he promises her he'll make the family business legitimate, he's unwilling to live his own life. His loyalty to the family has grown too important *(The Active Phase).*

All of this leads to Michael's Regression, where his father warns him of an assassination plot from within the family *(Regression)*. Shortly after, Vito dies, and a friend unknowingly reveals himself as the Corleone traitor. In response, Michael arranges for a series of high-profile murders. All four Dons of the rival families are killed, and even Michael's allies are marked for execution *(Choice)*. When Kay eventually confronts him, he denies his involvement—but, when three men arrive to pay respects to the new Don Corleone, he shuts his office door in her face *(The End)*.

Though Michael's inner struggle of loyalty might have seemed justified in the moment, it ultimately transforms him into a ruthless crime boss, sealing his fate as a negative arc.

Princess Nausicaä — The Flat Arc:

Finally, we come to Princess Nausicaä from Studio Ghibli's *Nausicaä of the Valley of the Wind.*

Nausicaä is the leader of a peaceful kingdom, surrounded on all sides by powerful neighbors and the Toxic Jungle—a slowly spreading forest of poisonous trees, gigantic insects, and death. This jungle is guarded by the Ohm, massive creatures that fly into a rage whenever they're threatened. Because of this, humans compete for space on the outskirts, hidden away in the few surviving parts of the world and constantly afraid that the Jungle's spores will destroy their homes next.

Nausicaä, however, is different. She walks freely through the Toxic Jungle, picking apart its secrets in the hope of one day healing her world. Deep down, she knows there's a reason the Jungle is spreading, and she believes that reason is the key to peace *(The Beginning)*. Of course, the people around her largely reject this truth, so Nausicaä pursues her research in secret—at least until an airship from the rival Tolmekian kingdom crashes in her valley. Soon after, the Tolmekian army arrives and Nausicaä is forced to trade her freedom for her people's protection *(Catalyst)*.

This is where Nausicaä's arc truly begins.

Through a series of trials, Nausicaä ends up captured aboard a Tolmekian airship, crash landing in the Toxic Jungle, and eventually stumbling upon a massive cavern deep beneath the jungle floor *(The Reactive Phase)*. Inside, the poison of the surface world is gone, instead replaced by clean water and air. This proves Nausicaä's truth is real. The Jungle isn't killing the world, but healing it. Peace really is possible *(Turning Point)*.

Now equipped with proof, Nausicaä sets out to share what she's learned. However, the world around her is still beset by violence. After being arrested by a rival kingdom, Nausicaä learns of their plan to trigger a stampede of Ohm, wiping out both her people and the Tolmekian army in one fell swoop *(The Active Phase)*. This forces Nausicaä to doubt her truth one final time—not whether it's real, but whether anyone will ever listen *(Regression)*.

Fortunately, Nausicaä refuses to abandon what she knows is right. Sneaking away, she races towards her valley, eventually putting herself between the stampede and her people. In doing so, she sacrifices herself to uphold her truth *(Choice)*. The Ohm spare her amid a glow of yellow light and the war comes to an end, fulfilling a prophecy that one day a hero would bring peace standing in a field of gold *(The End)*.

Ultimately, Nausicaä's journey isn't one of personal growth, but rather about healing the world around her. Though she certainly struggles with fear and doubt (and changes in subtle ways as a result) she never abandons her truth, even as her life seems to unravel. The result is a powerful flat arc!

Lessons from Chapter Five

Though we have many more journeys to explore throughout this book, these three arcs will come up again and again. No matter what type of character you're writing, one of these primary arcs will shape their transformation, determining whether they face a journey of growth, decay, or healing.

Because of this, these are a fantastic introduction to the world of character arcs.

Everything we'll discuss from here on out will build on the concepts from this chapter. After all, this book is about creating believable change. That change needs to happen organically, and these three arcs provide the perfect foundation for achieving that!

With that said, there is one path your characters could follow that turns these primary arcs on their head. Though it may seem strange now, not every story reaches a clear conclusion —leading to a whole category of characters that put an interesting twist on the positive, negative, and flat arc.

As unusual as these journeys might be, they're something you won't want to overlook. So, these "failed arcs" will be our focus for the next chapter.

In the meantime, here are a few questions to help you apply what you've learned to your cast:

- What does your character's life look like at the start of your story?
- How does this change by the end?

- Do they learn the right or wrong lessons during their journey?
- Is their story more about their own internal change or their effect on the world around them?

Once you've answered these questions, I'll see you in Chapter Six!

6

WHAT IF THEY FAIL?

Up until now, we've always assumed your characters would reach some kind of definitive conclusion.

They might grow, embrace their truth, and triumph over the conflict of their story. Perhaps they succumb to their inner struggle, decaying into a worse version of themselves. Or, maybe their story isn't about them at all, instead following them as they share their truth with the world around them.

But, what if there was another option?

What if your characters could *fail*?

Believe it or not, not all character arcs reach a clear endpoint, or at least not as clean cut as the ones we discussed in the previous chapter. Your characters will face a variety of hurdles throughout your story, and it's possible those hurdles will be too much for them to overcome. In these cases, your characters could get stuck in limbo, trapped in a form of stasis that denies them the true ending their arc was building towards.

So, let's take a moment to explore what failure really means in the world of character arcs.

When Characters Get Stuck

One of the most important parts of writing engaging novels is catharsis. This is a term we touched on back in Chapter One that describes the feeling of emotional satisfaction you get at the end of a good story. As you watch various conflicts, failures, and change unfold, that story builds emotional tension, which is then released when it reaches its finale.

This means catharsis and closure are closely related.

When you see a well-written character arc conclude, you feel emotionally satisfied, because the closure of that story creates catharsis. The journey that character went on has left a meaningful impact on their life, and you can see just how much their world has changed as a result. Even negative arcs, with their more tragic endings, still create this sense of catharsis thanks to the contrast they strike between where their characters begin and end.

Of course, everything I've just described was limited to you as the reader. You follow this character's journey, become invested in their success, and thus feel catharsis when their arc is over. However, catharsis isn't limited to us! Your cast will experience their own form of catharsis too.

Think of it this way: if the characters you're writing act and think like real people, it stands to reason that they'll feel emotional tension too—arguably even more strongly than you do, because they're actually *living* through these events. They're facing change, conflict, failure, and uncertainty, and when that journey comes to a close, they'll experience an intense wave of relief. The end of a story is an emotional time, not only for your readers, but for the characters they've come to love.

So, where do "failed" arcs come into this?

Well, what if your character never got to experience this catharsis? What if their story ended too soon, their arc was left incomplete, and they were trapped in stasis? In these cases, they'll never get the feeling of catharsis they're waiting for. They won't reach a definitive conclusion, and thus they'll be denied the cathartic resolution most characters get.

Basically, their arc will have failed.

This is not the same as the negative character arc. Though negative arcs are tragic, they still reach some clear outcome, unlike a failed arc. Instead, the "failed" arc is a modifier, one that can apply to any of the primary arcs we've studied.

The Failed Positive Arc:

Most positive arcs focus on a character facing their inner struggle, learning an important truth, and then acting on that truth in a final challenge.

However, life isn't always that simple.

It's possible your character's final challenge never comes, such as when another character resolves the conflict before your character can prove themselves. Alternatively, their truth might be more complicated than they believed. What if acting on their truth is the *wrong* decision? Though they understand this truth and want to reject their inner struggle, they also want to do the right thing, even when that conflicts with the lessons they've learned.

All of this leads to a character trapped in limbo. They've undeniably grown for the better, but they're also denied the catharsis needed to complete that transformation. Instead, they're stuck between their old inner struggle and their new truth—thus resulting in a failed positive arc.

The Failed Negative Arc:

Much like the positive arc, the negative arc is all about change, but with one important twist. Whereas the positive arc character grows for the better, the negative arc character devolves into their worst self. They're overwhelmed by their inner struggle, reject their truth, and become increasingly destructive as a result.

Meanwhile, there's another aspect of this arc to consider—and that is punishment.

This primary arc requires that your character suffers some consequence as a result of their negative transformation. This isn't about passing judgment, but about establishing stakes. Because their harmful actions affect both themselves and the people around them, those actions must create an equally negative reaction. Anakin murders Padme in *Revenge of the Sith,* bringing his worst fears to life, while Jay Gatsby is shot and killed in *The Great Gatsby.* These "punishments" complete these characters' arcs, making the consequences of their decay permanent and showing readers that their transformation is final.

The problem is, what happens if the negative arc character sees this punishment coming? What if this causes them to stop short?

I'm not talking about renouncing their inner struggle and accepting their truth in a moment of redemption, but rather about entering stasis. The failed negative arc character is undeniably worse than when they started, but they've also managed to hit the brakes. Perhaps another character finally convinces them to stop what they're doing, or maybe they see the writing on the wall.

Either way, they stop the runaway train that's so characteristic of the final moments of a negative arc—but, they never heal. Instead, they retreat into their shell, clinging to their flaws and failing their negative arc.

The Failed Flat Arc:

Finally, the flat arc is fairly easy to fail, because it highly depends on the rest of your cast.

A flat arc character must convince others of their truth in order to solve the core conflict of their story. Because of this, a failed flat arc character is one who never succeeds in this quest. They're never able to heal the inner struggle of their world, but they also refuse to abandon their truth. Instead, they're left in limbo, neither fulfilling their role as a flat arc nor decaying into a pseudo-negative arc.

A great example of this would be the "unicorn keeper" trope of old fairytales.

Someone with tremendous knowledge and wisdom is driven from society, because their world refuses to accept the lessons they have to share. However, instead of betraying their truth, they retreat into the forest. Here they protect the sparks of magic that might one day heal the wounds they failed to soothe. In doing so, they enter stasis—neither completing their flat arc nor giving in to the pressures of the outside world.

As you can see, failed arcs aren't just negative arcs by another name. Whereas negative arcs reach a definitive end point after the character hits rock bottom, *failed* negative characters are left in limbo. They're worse than when they started, but they haven't begun the process of redemption just yet—though, hopefully they will in the future!

Meanwhile, failed positive and flat arcs end in a similar state. These characters never get the catharsis of completing their journey, and are thus denied the satisfaction of reaching a clear conclusion.

Case Study: Shane

This is by far the most complex arc we've discussed so far, meaning now more than ever, we need some examples. So, for this chapter, let's take a look at the 1953 western *Shane*.

Named after its protagonist, this movie follows a lone cowboy as he wanders the hills of the American Midwest. Shane is mild-mannered and gracious, but he's also a terrifying force. He's incredibly skilled with a gun, and though he's careful not to discuss it, you can tell by how he avoids his past that he's done things he's deeply ashamed of.

This past returns to haunt Shane after he meets the Starretts.

The Starretts are a family of homesteaders who Shane stumbles upon through his travels. Though initially suspicious, they're kind to him, and Shane agrees to stay and help around the farm.

However, not everyone is happy with his presence. Shane is distinctly aware that he's an outsider, and this is made worse by the looming threat of Ryker—a dangerous rancher intent on taking the local land for himself.

As Ryker grows increasingly aggressive, Shane's arc is put to the test. Initially, he does his best to avoid conflict, afraid of returning to his violent past. However, during Shane's Regression, Ryker reveals his plans to murder Joe Starrett. Unable to stand by, Shane kills Ryker before fleeing back to the wilderness. With fresh blood on his hands, he no longer believes he belongs among the peaceful homesteaders.

Now, at first glance, this arc looks much like a positive arc—at least until the Regression makes things complicated.

Shane's inner struggle is his belief that killing and violence are shameful, no matter the reason. This is contrasted by his truth, that violence is a tool like any other. Rather than be ashamed of who he is, what matters is whether he uses his skills to do what's right.

This makes Shane's ending rather confusing. We the viewer understand his truth, and even Shane seems to recognize this lesson, going so far as to explain it to another character midway through the film.

So, why does Shane turn away and retreat to the wilderness?

Well, the answer is that he understood his truth, but never *accepted* it. Though he made the right choice in the end, he denied himself the catharsis and closure his arc needed, because he ended his story believing he had failed. That shame he started with never left him, even as he settled into his new life alongside the Starretts.

The result is a failed positive arc, one where Shane undeniably grew and learned, but where his final outcome left him trapped between his old inner struggle and his new truth.

NOTE: Shane's story is also a great example of the hermit's arc, which we'll explore later in Chapter Nine!

The Value of Failure

With that example in mind, let's wrap up by looking at where failed arcs fit among the primary arcs we've discussed.

As I've already mentioned, failed arcs are a modifier that layers on top of primary arcs. Your characters could follow a failed positive arc, failed negative arc, or failed flat arc, but never just a "failed" arc. You'll need some foundation to set their trajectory, even if that journey never reaches its true conclusion.

This allows for a few unique uses:

- **Bittersweet Finales:** In stories like *Shane,* the writers deny the character closure, even though readers know they made the right choice. This leaves a bittersweet taste in readers' mouths and is a great use of the failed positive arc in particular.
- **Preparing for Sequels:** If you're planning to continue your character's arc in a sequel, leaving them in limbo gives you room to return to them later on. Rather than resolve it and start a new arc in the next book, you can continue their transformation, or even take it in an entirely new direction. This isn't required for sequels, but it is a useful option.
- **Redemption Arcs:** Redemption arcs require your character to undergo some kind of negative arc before being redeemed. However, if your character gets *too* destructive, readers will have a hard time

> forgiving them. In these cases, a failed negative arc helps you hit the brakes before your character goes too far, while still allowing them to experience a clear downfall. We'll explore redemption arcs in more depth later in Chapter Twelve.

As useful as failed arcs are, they're also very delicate. A poorly written failed arc will usually feel like a story the writer just didn't know how to complete. The result is half-baked, whereas a good failed arc will still feel like it's reached its natural endpoint. Just like any other character, the failed character should still go through all eight stages of their arc, and should still make some clear choice that brings their story to an end.

The difference is the result of that choice. Rather than providing a definitive conclusion—either for better or worse—the failed arc character's choice leaves them stuck between their inner struggle and truth. They're unable to complete their journey, and thus unable to experience the feeling of catharsis they're looking for.

Of course, this doesn't mean failed arcs can deny readers their own catharsis.

Catharsis is a critical part of writing satisfying stories, which means your job is to give that emotional release to your readers regardless of your characters' outcomes. Because of this, failed arcs require a careful balance. Creating a strong resolution for your plot is usually the easiest way to bridge that gap. You might also balance your failed arcs with other complete arcs or with hints of a future story, giving your readers catharsis through other means.

In *Shane*, the writers managed this by relying on their plot more than on Shane himself. Shane definitively resolves the conflict threatening the homesteaders, even as his own transformation ends in limbo. Though viewers recognize the trap he's caught in, they're still happy to see him make the right choice, no matter how painful that choice might be.

Lessons from Chapter Six

In the end, failed arcs represent a more complicated side of storytelling. Though they aren't pure tragedies like the negative arc, they still have a tragic element, while also being hopeful and perhaps a bit bittersweet.

Like it or not, the human experience is complicated, and this means our characters need room to be complicated too. More than any of the three primary arcs we've studied, failed arcs highlight that complexity. Not all journeys have a clean endpoint. As writers, it's our duty to capture that on the page just like any other story.

One other way to fulfill this is through secondary arcs.

Throughout Part Two, we've been focused on primary arcs, but your characters could also experience a variety of "secondary" transformations too. So, as we move into Part Three, it's time to widen your options and delve even deeper into your characters' stories!

In the meantime, here are a few questions to help you apply what you've learned to your cast:

- Does your character end their story stuck between their truth and inner struggle?
- What traps them in this state of limbo?
- Do you plan to continue their arc in the future, or is this their true ending?

- How will you create catharsis for your readers, despite this failed arc?

Once you've answered these questions, I'll see you in Part Three!

III

TWELVE SECONDARY ARCS

"The fact of storytelling hints at a fundamental human unease, hints at human imperfection. Where there is perfection there is no story to tell."

BEN OKRI, NIGERIAN POET AND NOVELIST

7

THE HERO AND THE HEROINE

Though it might not seem like it now, this book was never meant to exist.

Believe it or not, *Mastering Character Arcs* was originally planned as a much smaller part of the first book in this series, *Write Your Hero*. That book is all about crafting powerful protagonists, and covers everything from the big picture role of the hero, to the finer details of their world, relationships, and even name. Naturally, *Write Your Hero* talks a lot about character arcs too—and that's where this book started to take shape.

As I was planning *Write Your Hero*, my focus was almost entirely on the classic hero archetype. However, as I delved deeper into that journey, I realized I was only looking at a slice of the bigger picture. Alongside this classic story were adventures of identity, independence, isolation, and age. While some characters set out to prove themselves, others learned to step back, handing off power to the next generation. Basically, I discovered secondary arcs, and the reality that this topic was far more complex than I had originally believed—and thus far more material than I could cover in *Write Your Hero* alone.

So, I shifted gears.

Write Your Hero became more focused, while *Mastering Character Arcs* took on a life of its own. After multiple months of work, I mapped out nearly a dozen secondary arcs for this book, far beyond the lonely hero I had originally envisioned. Though I was a bit overwhelmed at first, this shift ended up being a tremendous boon. *Mastering Character Arcs* expands on a lot of the things I could only touch on in *Write Your Hero* and opens up a whole world of possibilities that I can't help but be excited for!

Because of this, it only seems right to pay homage to the secondary arc that started it all: the hero.

This was the first secondary arc I truly understood, and though I didn't realize it back then, it was the key I needed to unlock a much deeper understand of character arcs. The hero is where this book's journey began, so it's also where we'll begin our discussion of secondary arcs!

Earning Their Title

As a quick refresher, secondary arcs are a specialized type of character arc, focused on specific journeys like coming of age or redemption. These universal journeys are optional, but they do combine with primary arcs to create a lot of interesting possibilities—something we'll explore further towards the end of Part Three.

In total, we'll be discussing twelve secondary arcs in this book, starting with the hero and the heroine.

The hero's arc and the heroine's arc are somewhat unique in the world of secondary arcs, in that they function as mirror images. Both follow the same basic patterns, but focus on very different aspects of the classic "hero's journey."

We'll start with the similarities first.

These two character arcs are what most people think of when they imagine a traditional hero, following a character on a cyclical journey away from home, into the unknown, and back again. Along the way, the hero and the heroine go through three, distinct phases:

- **Starting in the Known World:** The hero and heroine begin in their normal world. This represents stability, the status quo, and the "known," though there are undeniable flaws lingering at the edges. Most (though not all) heroes are discontent in their known world, even if they appreciate the safety and security it provides.
- **Facing the Unknown:** This shifts when the hero and heroine enter the unknown, a magical, frightening place filled with possibility. Often, this unknown will be a literal place, though it could also be a simple change in your character's circumstances. Either way, this is where they'll face tests and trials that help them attain mastery of their new world, eventually equipping them with the tools or wisdom they need to take charge of their story.
- **Returning to the Known:** Finally, the hero and heroine return to the known. By now, they fully understand the known's flaws, and use that understanding to heal the wounds of their world. In the process, they become a hero, safeguarding their community and ensuring its future for years to come.

It's this return phase that makes these characters true heroes. By sacrificing their place in the unknown world to share the rewards of their journey, they not only lift up their society, but earn the title of hero too.

This is distinct from a normal positive arc. While the positive arc character is content to grow and evolve within themselves, the hero and the heroine must use their transformation to better their society. Though the positive arc character likely will improve the world around them, it isn't their story's focus—while it's essential here.

Of course, the hero and the heroine's arcs are separate journeys for a reason.

The hero's arc is focused on your character's *external* journey, while the heroine is more concerned with their *internal* journey. Both start out in their known worlds suffering from a deep inner struggle. However, the hero sets out into the unknown in search of a physical reward, along with mastery over their external world:

- **The Beginning:** The hero starts their story suffering from some inner struggle. Meanwhile, their community is suffering too. Though they might not realize it just yet, a powerful threat is brewing beneath the surface—both within and outside their known world.
- **Catalyst:** This threat reveals itself at the Catalyst, forcing the hero to leave their known world and enter the unknown in search of the tools they need to overcome this conflict.
- **The Reactive Phase:** Once in the unknown, the hero will face a variety of challenges, learning and adapting as they struggle to get their bearings. Along

the way, they'll begin to understand the flaws of their community, though they won't know how to handle those flaws just yet.

- **Turning Point:** This culminates in a major test, where the hero embraces their truth and receives a reward. This could be anything from a new skill to key allies, powers, or physical tools. Whatever it is, it's rarely what the hero expected when they began their quest.
- **The Active Phase:** Now comfortable in the unknown world, the hero will dread returning home. They've attained mastery over the unknown, and are hesitant to leave that all behind. Instead, they make plans to resolve their story's conflict without abandoning the unknown world.
- **Regression:** Unfortunately, this plan falls though. After a major defeat, the hero is forced to question their place in the unknown, as well as the fate of their known world. If either is to survive, they must sacrifice their own desires in order to protect them.
- **Choice:** Realizing their reward is the secret to saving their community, the hero makes the choice to leave the unknown and return home. In a final test, they share their reward and sacrifice a part of themselves for the greater good, earning the title of hero.
- **The End:** With their community safe, the hero is left with a foot in both worlds. No longer restricted to one or the other, they bridge the gap between the known and unknown.

As an example, a character like Disney's Mulan perfectly embodies this hero's quest. She sets out to protect her family, struggles to find her place in the Chinese army, defeats the warlord threatening her country, and finally returns home with honor. Though she learns a lot about herself and overcomes an inner struggle along the way, her story is primarily about facing physical threats and thus attaining physical mastery.

Meanwhile, the heroine takes a different approach.

This character starts out in the same known world, suffering from the same inner struggle—but, rather than set out on a physical quest, they leave home in search of their true self. This means the heroine's journey is all about wisdom, identity, and internal connections:

- **The Beginning:** The heroine starts their story suffering from some inner struggle, taking shape as a deep emotional disconnect within themselves. Meanwhile, their community is suffering too. Though they might not realize it just yet, a powerful threat is brewing beneath the surface—both within and outside their known world.
- **Catalyst:** This threat reveals itself at the Catalyst, forcing the heroine to leave their known world and enter the unknown in search of the wisdom needed to protect their people.
- **The Reactive Phase:** Once in the unknown world, the heroine will face a variety of challenges, learning and adapting as they struggle to shed the weight of their old identities. Along the way, they'll begin to understand the flaws of their community, though they won't know how to handle those flaws just yet.
- **Turning Point:** This culminates in a major test, where the heroine embraces their truth and rekindles their connection with their true self. This internal change is typically represented by some

symbolic action, signaling that the heroine has attained a deeper wisdom.

- **The Active Phase:** Now comfortable in the unknown world, the heroine will dread returning home, unsure how to reconcile their old self with their new identity. Instead, they make plans to resolve their story's conflict without abandoning the unknown, afraid of what the known world represents.
- **Regression:** Unfortunately, this plan falls though. After a major defeat, the heroine is forced to question their new identity, as well as the fate of their known world. If their community is to survive, they must accept who they are without fear.
- **Choice:** Realizing this wisdom is the secret to saving their community, the heroine makes the choice to leave the unknown and return home. In a final test, they share what they've learned and sacrifice a part of themselves for the greater good, earning the title of heroine.
- **The End:** With their community safe, the heroine is left with a foot in both worlds. No longer restricted to one or the other, they bridge the gap between the known and unknown, finally at peace with who they are.

You can see this heroine's arc at work in Disney's *Moana*.

Much like Mulan, Moana sets out into the unknown to protect her family. However, her story isn't about physical mastery. Though she absolutely faces physical trials, her triumph is instead discovering her ancestry and accepting her emotional bond with the ocean. It's this deeper understanding of herself and her world that allows her to save her people and rekindle her spirit, marking her as a heroine.

THE HERO VS. THE HEROINE

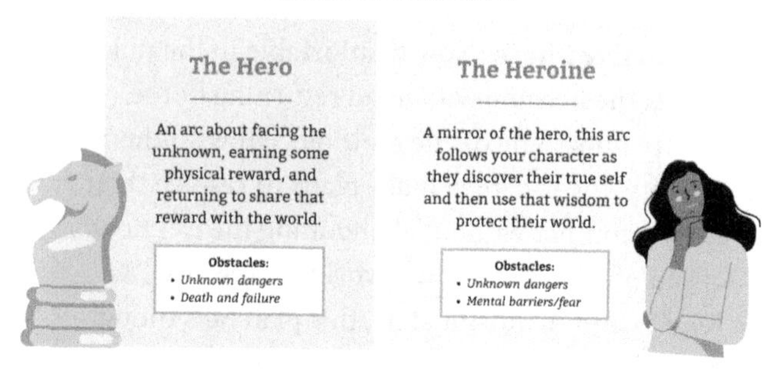

Now, I mentioned the "hero's journey" a moment ago, and this was done on purpose. If you're at all familiar with the world of story structure, you've probably run into the Hero's Journey before, meaning these arcs might sound familiar.

For those who don't know, the Hero's Journey is a story structure based on the work of American professor Joseph Campbell. Campbell is perhaps best known for his theory of the monomyth, which is the idea that all human mythology is based on the same core patterns—that being the journey into the unknown, the facing of symbolic trials, and the eventual return to the known. These patterns culminate in the crowning of a hero, charged with preserving the community and safeguarding its future for the next generation.

As you can probably guess, this Hero's Journey is the inspiration for the hero's arc we just discussed. However, the heroine's arc is another story.

As great as Campbell's work is, he had a major blind spot when it came to less traditional, introspective stories. The Hero's Journey is tightly intertwined with physical quests, physical mastery, and physical rewards, but what about more internal journeys?

Fortunately, those who came after Campbell picked up the slack—specifically Maureen Murdock's *The Heroine's Journey*.

Murdock and other authors like Victoria Lynn Schmidt took the basic structure laid out by Campbell and modified it into something welcoming of more spiritual and emotional journeys. This fills the gaps left by the Hero's Journey, and is why I refer to these two secondary arcs as "hero" and "heroine."

No matter which of these two arcs you're interested in, I encourage you to read up on these journeys if you'd like to learn more. Though they're technically a form of story structure, they still have a lot to offer when it comes to character development, and this isn't the last time I'll mention them throughout this book.

NOTE: Though the words "hero" and "heroine" have gendered connotations, these arcs can apply to any character. While Campbell and Murdock might have envisioned them as being gender-specific, female heroes and male heroines are absolutely possible!

Of course, not all "heroes" follow the hero or heroine's arc. While these arcs might share a name with your protagonist, that doesn't mean every protagonist is the right fit for these journeys. After all, these are secondary character arcs (and thus optional) for a reason!

Case Study: Ashitaka and Paikea Apirana

With those secondary arcs in mind, let's look at how these journeys unfold in practice, based on two movies:

- *Princess Mononoke* (1997)
- *Whale Rider* (2002)

These two films will make for interesting examples, because they actually focus on a variation of these arcs—specifically, the flat hero's arc and the flat heroine's arc.

Thus far, we've been focusing on only the positive versions of these two arcs, but every secondary arc we study will also include negative and flat versions. This is something we'll explore further later in Part Three. In the meantime, just remember that secondary arcs build on top of primary arcs, and that in this case, those primary arcs are flat.

Ashitaka — The Hero's Arc:

We'll start things off with Ashitaka, the flat hero of the animated movie *Princess Mononoke.*

Ashitaka begins his story like many fantasy heroes, settled into life as a guard in a peaceful village. His truth is one of peace, and he believes in striking a balance between humanity and nature. However, not all is well. The kingdoms of men are slowly falling to disease and war, and though his people haven't been affected yet, the spectre of death lingers over the horizon *(The Beginning).* This spectre eventually arrives in the form of Nago, the demon boar. Early one morning, Nago attacks Ashitaka's village, caught in a blind rage—and though Ashitaka kills him, he himself is cursed in the process. Knowing he'll slowly decay as the curse spreads, he's forced to leave his village behind, heading west in hopes of being cured by the powerful Deer God *(The Catalyst).*

This begins Ashitaka's journey into the unknown.

While searching for the Deer God's forest, Ashitaka tackles difficult terrain, skirts along the edges of brutal battles, and eventually meets the leader of the Ironworks, Lady Eboshi. Eboshi is a complicated figure, responsible for both the safety of her people, as well as a raging war between humans and the nature gods. She represents the opposite of Ashitaka's truth, and though he appreciates all she does for her kingdom, he can't overlook her cruelty *(The Reactive Phase)*.

After a tour of the Ironworks, Ashitaka decides it's time to leave. However, before he gets the chance, Eboshi is attacked by the daughter of the wolf gods, Princess Mononoke. Unwilling to let the two kill each other, Ashitaka steps in, ending up mortally wounded in the process. As thanks, Mononoke carries him to the Deer God, who heals him—but doesn't lift his curse *(Turning Point)*.

Oddly enough, this is Ashitaka's "reward." Though he's crushed by the realization that the Deer God won't help him, it also solidifies his decision to stop the war. From here on out, his own safety is less important, and his truth takes center stage. He sets out to convince those around him that humanity and nature can coexist *(The Active Phase)*.

This comes to a head when Ashitaka realizes Lady Eboshi is headed for the Deer God, intent on killing it. Despite his best efforts, his truth is dismissed, and the war rages on *(Regression)*. Fortunately, he refuses to surrender. When Eboshi beheads the Deer God and unleashes a horrific demon, Ashitaka and Mononoke work together to track down the Deer God's head and return it, thus appeasing its spirit *(Choice)*. Through this, Ashitaka proves his truth once and for all. His curse is lifted, and he begins his new life in the Ironworks, acting as a bridge between the known world of men and the unknown world of nature *(The End)*. In doing so, he not only gains physical strength, but also the title of hero.

Pai Apirana — The Heroine's Arc:

In contrast to Ashitaka, Pai's heroine's journey is much more subdued.

Pai is young Māori girl living on an isolated island as the sole grandchild of her village's chief. She was originally a twin, but both her twin brother and mother died when she was born. Paralyzed by grief, her father abandoned her with her grandparents.

Twelve years later, and Pai has become a complicated figure. Her grandfather Koro loves her deeply, but she also represents the destruction of his bloodline. Without a male heir, the tribe is rudderless, and Koro's own bitterness prevents him from fulfilling his role as chief. Through all of this, Pai has done her best to keep the peace. Though she's hurt by her grandfather's anger, she knows that this is her home, and that she can preserve its traditions just as much as any boy *(The Beginning)*.

This relationship begins to shift when her father returns home. Koro is elated, thinking his son will finally take up the mantle of leadership, but Pai's father is really there to take Pai away. Initially, she's torn, but eventually she tells him no; she won't leave her home *(Catalyst)*.

From here, Pai's journey shifts into the unknown world of tradition. Koro, having realized his son will never come back, decides it's time to find a new leader. He begins training the village boys, while growing increasingly cold towards Pai. Though he warns her not to interfere, she's stubborn, and slowly learns from the sidelines *(The Reactive Phase)*. Unfortunately, Koro's teaching proves ineffective.

None of the boys are making progress, and so Koro calls to the whale gods for guidance. Pai calls as well, and though Koro hears nothing, she hears their voices call back—confirming that she's the leader of her tribe *(Turning Point)*.

Now confident she's on the right path, Pai decides she needs to prove her worth to her grandfather. Eventually, she retrieves a whale tooth from the bottom of the ocean, marking her as her tribe's next leader *(The Active Phase)*. She plans to tell Koro later that evening, but disaster strikes instead. A pod of whales are found beached on the island. If they aren't returned to the ocean soon, they'll die, striking a painful blow to the tribe. As the situation grows worse, Koro turns on Pai. In his anger, he claims she brings nothing but misery and grief *(Regression)*.

At this point, it would be easy for Pai to surrender—but, her truth remains.

Realizing she has the wisdom needed to restore her tribe's spirit, she makes a symbolic return, climbing onto the back of the largest whale and gently guiding it towards the ocean. As she does, the others follow, and Pai disappears with the pod beneath the waves *(Choice)*. Sometime later, she wakes up in the hospital, with Koro holding her hand. He pleads for her forgiveness, and she's heralded as the new leader of her village, loved by both her people and the grandfather she cares so much about *(The End)*.

Though Pai is just a child, she ends her journey as a powerful flat heroine, leading her community to a new era of prosperity—much like Ashitaka does in his story.

Still, each of these stories take a slightly different perspective.

While Ashitaka's journey is all about his fight to gain physical strength, allies, and remedies, Pai's quest is one of wisdom and identity. In the process, Ashitaka embodies the hero, while Pai represents the heroine. This happens in concert with their primary arcs. Alongside their unique secondary arcs, both Ashitaka and Pai undergo flat arcs, following them as they use their truths to soothe the wounds of their world. When combined, you end up with two powerful films featuring two equally compelling characters!

Lessons from Chapter Seven

As we wrap up this chapter, I want to reinforce the ways secondary arcs differ from primary arcs one final time.

At first glance, I wouldn't blame you for conflating the two, or for assuming the hero and heroine are just "fancier" primary arcs. However, I'd argue this misses the bigger picture. What makes these arcs so valuable is that they provide an extra layer of depth beyond the basic positive, negative, or flat arc. To undergo a primary arc, your characters don't have to follow this cyclical journey. They never have to undergo a shift into the unknown or a return to the known, and thus never have to share the lessons they've learned with their community.

It's this return that sets the hero and heroine apart from other characters, elevating them into a secondary arc of their own.

Of course, they're far from the only secondary arc you have to choose from! From the elder's arc to the redemption arc, we have a lot of ground left to cover—with each arc only expanding the many paths your characters could take.

In the meantime, here are a few questions to help you apply what you've learned to your cast:

- Does your character leave their known world behind and venture into the unknown?
- If their arc focused primarily on physical mastery or internal wisdom?
- Do they eventually make the choice to return and help their community?
- How will they ultimately earn the title of hero or heroine?

Once you've answered these questions, I'll see you in Chapter Eight!

8

THE PROBLEMS WITH DESTINY

Destiny and fate are tricky things…

On the one hand, they often come with interesting abilities, cool perks, and tremendous power; but they can also leave our characters unsure of who they really are. If their life wasn't dictated by prophecy, what would be left? Who are they beneath that mask? Even worse, what if their fate runs counter to everything they believe?

Combine this inner turmoil with the difficult process of growing up, and you have the perfect storm for a whole variety of powerful, cathartic conflicts. So, in this chapter, let me introduce you to two secondary arcs that explore the younger side of your cast—along with all the problems that come from destiny!

Coming of Age and the Chosen One

The hero and the heroine from the previous chapter were relatively straightforward compared to some of the arcs we'll be studying throughout this book. With that foundation set, it's time to delve into two more complex arcs: the coming of age arc and the chosen one's arc!

Both of these arcs represent a "younger" side of storytelling, focusing on characters as they come to terms with their future and the difficult process of growing up. Because of this, these arcs are often paired together. Characters like Aang from *Avatar: The Last Airbender* or Anakin Skywalker from the *Star Wars* prequels both represent the kind of dual coming of age/chosen one journeys that are endemic throughout YA, fantasy, and science fiction stories.

Despite this, these two arcs are fundamentally different.

The coming of age arc is built around the bildungsroman, following a character as they undergo the shift from dependent child to independent adult. Along the way, they'll have to prove they're capable of handling the adult world, develop their own individual identity, and learn to be self-reliant, even as other characters try to hold them back:

- **The Beginning:** Your character begins their story suffering from some inner struggle, as well as from the control of their guardians. Even if they love their guardian figures, they're beginning to chafe against their rules and expectations.
- **Catalyst:** Eventually, they've had enough. Some event causes a shift in their life, opening the door for them to pull away from their guardians and set out into the adult world.
- **The Reactive Phase:** Here they must learn to fend for themselves, navigating despite their own inexperience and their inner struggle. In the process, they'll have to fight against characters who seek to

exploit them, as well as their guardians' attempts to pull them back into the child world.

- **Turning Point:** This reaches its peak in the form of a major test, where your character will have the chance to reject their role as child. They've tasted independence, meaning now they must establish their new identity as an adult through some rebellious act.
- **The Active Phase:** From there, your character becomes more confident in the adult world, allowing them to assert their independence. However, their inner struggle is still festering beneath the surface—and being an adult isn't all benefits.
- **Regression:** This culminates in a painful defeat. Confronted by the dangers of the adult world, your character will question whether they can truly survive on their own, or if they should give in and return to the child world.
- **Choice:** If they're to succeed, they'll have to reject the security of childhood and instead face the consequences of their new independence. In doing so, they'll embrace their truth, allowing them to resolve your story's conflict and complete their arc.
- **The End:** Their journey ends as they come of age. They've demanded to be respected as an equal member of the adult world, and they've earned that right. From now on, they'll no longer be restricted by the role of child.

What makes this coming of age arc particularly interesting is that it isn't limited to literal children, even if that's where it's most common.

Many stories feature this journey of independence, from:

- Children individuating from their parents or family
- Characters learning to live alone after their partners pass away
- Teenagers leaving their village to prove themselves
- Or immigrants establishing their independence in a new country

A great example of this is Rose from the movie *Titanic.*

In that movie, Rose is an adult, but she starts her journey trapped under the thumb of her abusive fiancé. Though she may not be a child, she's living in a "child world," unable to make her own decisions and instead trading autonomy for safety. As her arc unfolds, she'll eventually reject this child world, demanding independence and eventually accepting the dangers of being on her own.

COMING OF AGE VS. THE CHOSEN ONE

Coming of Age

An arc about growing into an independent adult. To succeed in this arc, your character will have to earn a place in the adult world.

Obstacles:
- *The rules of childhood*
- *Predators/authority*

The Chosen One

An arc about accepting our destiny. Your character will have to come to terms with fate (and how it affects their life) to complete their arc.

Obstacles:
- *Heavy expectations*
- *Fate vs. identity/desire*

Meanwhile, the chosen one's arc is all about coming to terms with destiny. This arc follows a character as they're warned of their fate, struggle to live up to it, and eventually learn to balance their own needs with the demands and expectations of the world around them:

- **The Beginning:** Your character begins their story suffering from some inner struggle. Though many chosen ones coast through life thanks to traits or skills they don't fully understand, this harmful belief still leaves them discontent and uneasy.
- **Catalyst:** This begins to change after their fate is revealed, shattering the stability of their normal world and upending their perception of themselves.
- **The Reactive Phase:** Overwhelmed by the expectations of others, your character will have to come to grips with their new role, changing relationships, and sudden revelation. This phase brings a lot of pressure as your character struggles to understand what their destiny truly means.
- **Turning Point:** Eventually, they'll master a key part of their abilities thanks to a major test, overcoming some hurdle and thus embracing their fate (and truth) in a new way.
- **The Active Phase:** From there, they'll start to have more faith in themselves, leaning into their newfound skills as they work to resolve their story's conflict. Still, they likely have lingering reservations about what their destiny is asking of them—combining with their inner struggle to leave them on shaky ground.
- **Regression:** This culminates in a major defeat, where the chosen one will be forced to question who they are, if their fate was right in the first place, and whether they can truly fulfill it.
- **Choice:** In order to succeed, they'll have to overcome these fears, embracing their truth and thus gaining mastery over their destiny. Their fate will come to pass, though often in ways they never expected.
- **The End:** Thanks to their journey, their world will

begin to heal and they'll guide their society back into balance, fulfilling their job as the chosen one.

With that said, despite this arc's name, having a destiny doesn't automatically lead to a chosen one's arc.

This secondary arc is specifically about the struggle to *accept* fate, meaning your character will need to have reservations about their future. In these cases, your character's destiny might run counter to their own desires, ask for impossible results, or push them to do things they know they would regret. These doubts and fears turn their fate into something of an internal enemy. They'll have to fight within themselves to understand what their destiny means, balance that destiny with who they are, and figure out what they're truly capable of—otherwise, they risk going down a dark path.

Case Study: Jim Hawkins and Neo

Unlike some of the secondary arcs we'll explore later, there's no shortage of these two arcs.

Because the coming of age and chosen one's arcs are well suited to stories of growth, learning, and maturity, they're practically required in genres saturated with young readers —meaning there are hundreds if not thousands of options to choose from!

For this chapter, we'll be focusing on two popular films:

- *Treasure Planet* (2002)
- *The Matrix* (1999)

Jim Hawkins — The Coming of Age Arc:

Jim Hawkins from *Treasure Planet* is your classic troublesome teenager.

As a young boy, his father abandoned him to travel the galaxy, and Jim has been bitter ever since. Now older, he feels trapped by his life. By day, he works in his mother's failing inn, before running out to skysurf at night. Though his mother tries to rein him in, he's no stranger to the law, and is almost constantly being arrested *(The Beginning)*.

One evening, an old pilot cashes his spaceship just outside the inn, and Jim rushes to save him. In return, the dying pilot gives Jim a map. Soon after, pirates attack, and Jim realizes the map leads to the famed Treasure Planet. After much convincing, he gets his mother's permission to search for the treasure, and sets out on his adventure *(The Catalyst)*.

To travel through space, Jim needs a ship, and so he enlists the help of a captain. However, though he brought them the map, he ends up relegated to kitchen duty. The other sailors look down on him, and Jim resents being treated like a child. The one exception is John Silver, the ship's cook. Slowly, Silver and Jim develop something of a pseudo father-son relationship, even as Silver hides his true identity as a murderous pirate *(The Reactive Phase)*. This comes to light when they approach Treasure Planet. Jim overhears Silver insisting that he won't impede the crew's plans and that their relationship is only fake—though he's really lying to protect Jim's life. Heartbroken, Jim rebels against Silver, stealing the map and escaping the ship with the captain before crash landing on the planet below *(Turning Point)*.

Once there, Jim decides to find the treasure on his own, without the security of Silver *(The Active Phase)*. Eventually, he succeeds, only to realize Silver has captured the captain. Using her as leverage, he forces Jim to hand over the map—reinforcing his betrayal *(Regression).*

Of course, like all treasures, the island is booby trapped.

After tripping an alarm, the planet begins to self-destruct, taking the crew with it. With their deaths looming over them, Jim and Silver realize they're allies after all, and the two work together to get everyone to safety in the nick of time—openly respecting each other as equals *(Choice).*

With their adventures at an end, Jim returns home, now an accepted member of the adult world. The treasure he found is used to save his mother's inn, and he and Silver develop a healthy understanding. Though Silver refuses to stay, he and Jim leave on good terms, with Jim no longer feeling the sense of abandonment he used to struggle with *(The End).*

From now on, he's secure in his independence, completing his coming of age arc!

Neo — The Chosen One's Arc:

When compared to Jim, Neo is markedly older, though he still represents a relatively "young" perspective.

Neo is the protagonist of *The Matrix,* and starts his story as a dejected hacker, trapped beneath the grind of the modern world. Unhappy with his life, he feverishly pursues messages left for him by "The Matrix," all while dodging government officials and trying to fly below their radar (*The Beginning*).

This becomes difficult when Neo is brought before a man named Morpheus. Morpheus reveals he was the one sending Neo the messages, and presents him with a choice: either forget everything, or learn the truth of his existence. Neo chooses to learn (*Catalyst*). In the process, it's revealed that his life is a simulation. In the real world, humans are being farmed for their energy, while their minds are trapped in the Matrix to keep them numb. Neo, meanwhile, is "The One," a mythical figure destined to end the Matrix and free humanity (*The Reactive Phase*).

Naturally, this is a big realization, and Neo struggles to adapt to his new identity as he slowly masters his abilities. In a mock fight with Morpheus, Neo overpowers him, and Morpheus confidently declares that he was right. Neo really is "The One" (*Turning Point*).

Of course, with such a heavy destiny, there are bound to be lingering doubts. When Neo is brought before the Oracle, she warns him that he might not be who he believes—and that he'll eventually have to choose between his life and Morpheus'. This comes to pass when the group is betrayed, leading to Morpheus' capture by AI agents (*The Active Phase*). Trapped between the real world and the Matrix, Neo is helpless as his friends are systematically killed. Though he survives, he realizes his status as "The One" means nothing in the real world (*Regression*).

Eventually, Neo lets go of his fears and returns to save Morpheus. By embracing his abilities and the destiny they stem from, Neo defeats the powerful forces controlling the Matrix, lending new life to the human rebellion (*Choice*). This ends with a scene of Neo inside the Matrix, declaring his intent to free all of humanity (*The End*).

This is a classic chosen one's arc, and it ends in a classic way.

Though Neo appears to die during his Regression, he's resurrected, rising to meet his destiny. While not all chosen ones follow this exact pattern of resurrection, many do—making Neo's journey a great example of a typical chosen one.

Lessons from Chapter Eight

Before we wrap up this chapter, I want to quickly address some problems unique to the chosen one's arc.

This secondary arc tends to be fraught with challenges, primarily because it's so easy to get wrong. The idea of having to fulfill some predetermined destiny is often antithetical to the concepts of failure and change required for a successful arc—and thus for writing a cathartic character. Because fate is on their side, there's no reason to fear that character will ever stumble, make mistakes, or grow much at all. If their destiny determines everything they do, their choices don't matter, and their victory is predetermined.

You can see this mistake in a character like Rey from the *Star Wars* sequel trilogy. Though she had tremendous potential, her character represents the chosen one gone wrong. She's destined by her bloodline to become a powerful Jedi, and the writers used this as an excuse to gloss over the many challenges, trials, and struggles a character needs to feel dynamic. The result is that Rey never really grows, despite following what was presumably meant to be a positive arc. The same goes—ironically—for Anakin Skywalker. Though he's a great example of a negative primary arc, his secondary chosen one's arc is as flat as a sheet of paper.

So, how can you avoid these pitfalls when writing a chosen one of your own?

Well, fortunately, the eight stages of this arc should go a long way towards helping you create meaningful conflict for your character. However, you'll also want to consider a few additional things to make sure your chosen one undergoes a cathartic transformation.

Make Them Struggle:

Even if wielding some power is their destiny, it should take time to master those abilities. In the meantime, let them struggle as they adapt to their new role.

Give Them Flaws:

Just like other characters, your chosen one will need a clear inner struggle to fight against throughout their arc. Leverage this struggle to ensure their victory isn't easy.

Ask Questions:

A major part of the chosen one's arc is accepting their destiny—but, before they do so, they'll have questions. They might doubt their abilities, or maybe they reject their fate entirely. Either way, don't be afraid to have your character question their journey.

Consider the Risk:

Because the chosen one is often an overused archetype, you have less room to play with difficult or unsavory characters. Above all, you need to make your chosen one likable if you want readers to follow their story.

Motivate Them:

We discussed story goals at length back in Part One, and these are important for every character you write—but especially for a chosen one. When choosing their story goal, make sure you give them motivations that are personal, beyond just fulfilling their destiny.

Make Them Matter: Your chosen one should be the only character who can fulfill their destiny, not because it's "theirs," but because they alone have the wisdom, perspective, or traits needed to succeed.

Leverage Your Cast:

While this might not work for every story, chosen one characters often benefit from large supporting casts. These other characters add depth to their journey, and give readers someone to root for beyond the chosen one.

Leave Fate Uncertain:

Finally, I encourage you to make your character's fate uncertain. Even if you know they'll succeed, it doesn't hurt for your readers to be left wondering!

Luckily, the coming of age arc doesn't include quite as many opportunities for mishaps as the chosen one—so, no further warnings needed!

In the meantime, here are a few questions to help you apply what you've learned to your cast:

- Will your character have to leave behind their child world and enter adulthood?
- How does their child world restrict them early in their character arc?
- Is their journey about facing their destiny and the many challenges that come with it?
- If so, how can you ensure they earn their victories, rather than having success handed to them?

Once you've answered these questions, I'll see you in Chapter Nine!

9

SURVIVING IN THE WILDERNESS

The world can be a scary place—especially when you're on your own.

Having friends and allies by our side takes the edge off our adventures, providing support and advice when we need it most. Mentors teach us how to navigate the world, while guardians keep us safe. Even our enemies have a role to play! Adversaries and rivals can be a powerful force pushing us forward, testing our will and giving us something to struggle against. Though we might try to deny it, the people around us shape nearly every aspect of our lives.

The same will be true for our characters.

So far, we've been focused on characters who start their story as part of a larger community. That community might be a kingdom or tribe, or it may simply be a family or friend group. Whatever it looks like, it provides the initial push your characters need to begin their arcs, as well as moments of conflict and comfort as their journeys unfold. Whether they're leaving their childhood guardians in search of independence or struggling to understand their true self, their community is a vital piece of their adventure.

All of this raises an important question... What about characters who lack this community? What about those who exist on the edges of society, or who have abandoned the human world entirely?

Well, that is the domain of our next two secondary arcs: the hermit and the rogue.

The Hermit and the Rogue

Out of all twelve secondary arcs in this book, the hermit and the rogue are by far my favorites!

Not only do they create some fascinating, often unorthodox characters, but they're also the first real departure from the classic hero mythos we've studied thus far. Rather than leaving the village to face the unknown, both the hermit and the rogue start their stories on the fringes of their society, or even outside of that society altogether. As a result, these arcs are about reentering the human world, finding stability and security in a place neither the hermit nor rogue feel entirely comfortable in.

Of course, these are two distinct arcs—and, much like the hero and heroine from Chapter Seven, they both take a slightly different perspective on this "outcast" archetype.

First on our list, the hermit starts their story living in the literal or metaphorical wilderness. They're isolated from the people around them, and so their arc is about returning to the "human world." Along the way, they'll have to reconcile the wounds and experiences that originally drove them away with their new role in their community. You can actually see this at work in a story we touched on earlier in this book! Shane represents the classic hermit's arc, returning to live among people after an untold time in the wilderness:

- **The Beginning:** The hermit begins their story suffering from some deep inner struggle, which keeps them isolated from their community. Though they've accepted this isolation on the surface, they can't help but feel discontent.
- **Catalyst:** This stasis is broken when the hermit makes contact with someone from their old world. Usually, this person will be seeking the hermit's help, though sometimes they arrive in the hermit's life for other reasons. Either way, they'll coax the hermit to return to their community, thus embroiling them in the conflict of their story.
- **The Reactive Phase:** Of course, the hermit will initially resist. The baggage of their past will make it hard to reenter society, especially as old wounds come to the surface. Despite these wounds, they'll slowly find reasons to care for their community.
- **Turning Point:** This culminates in a major test, where the hermit will prove to both themselves and others that they belong in the human world.
- **The Active Phase:** Now more comfortable, the hermit sets their sights on resolving the conflict of their story. However, they haven't fully accepted their new world, or forgiven the wounds that drove them away in the first place.
- **Regression:** These wounds return at the Regression, when the hermit faces a painful defeat. Their place in

the human world will be called into question, and they'll realize they can't run from the past after all.

- **Choice:** Eventually, either the hermit or their community will atone for the past, giving the hermit the push they need to accept their truth—as well as resolve the conflict threatening their human world.
- **The End:** With their world now secure, the hermit establishes themselves as a full member of their community, no longer isolated in the wilderness.

In contrast to the hermit, the rogue begins their journey already connected to their society—though that link is only tenuous. The rogue doesn't have the luxury of leaving the human world behind, and is instead trapped on the fringes of their community. This is the domain of pirates, bastards, widows, and the destitute. Because of their fragile position, their journey is about finding belonging in a world that has no place for them.

THE HERMIT VS. THE ROGUE

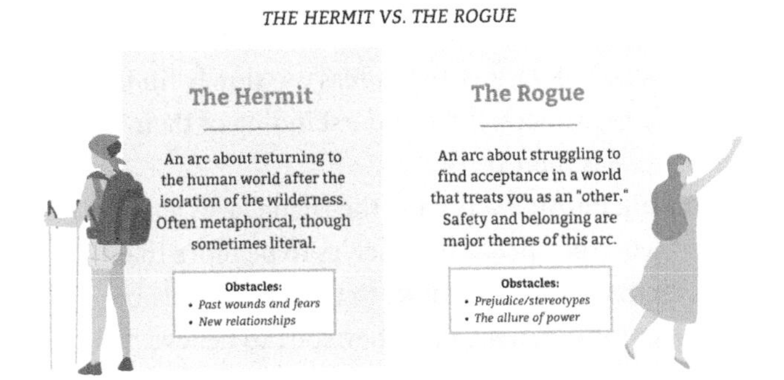

Continuing with our theme of westerns, the 1939 movie *Stagecoach* features an excellent example of this rogue's arc.

Dallas is a prostitute who starts her story run out of town by the local "Law and Order League." However, despite their cruelty, Dallas has a good heart. Through a variety of twists, turns, and difficult choices, she eventually learns to let go of her self-hatred and instead find belonging with a man who loves her for who she is—not for how other people see her:

- **The Beginning:** The rogue begins on the fringes of society. They're seen as illegitimate, and thus denied the security most people enjoy. Instead, they cling to other forms of power or fall prey to predators as they struggle to protect themselves the best they can.
- **Catalyst:** This delicate balance is broken when some conflict arrives that threatens the last scraps of security the rogue has. Alternatively, someone may promise them a way out of their current situation, luring them into the open. Either way, the rogue makes the choice to take that risk.
- **The Reactive Phase:** Unfortunately, they're immediately rejected or ridiculed by the people around them, leaving the rogue with little to no support. Despite this, they press on, slowly finding allies and growing their understanding of their world —as well as their truth.
- **Turning Point:** Eventually the rogue faces a major test. Here they prove themselves to be more than their circumstances thanks to their truth, earning respect for the first time. They start to believe there really is a way out of their situation.
- **The Active Phase:** From here, the rogue becomes more confident, demanding an equal place within their society. However, they haven't addressed their inner struggle just yet, or let go of the idea that they're illegitimate.

- **Regression:** This culminates in a major defeat, where some event proves that the rogue is still unwanted. Deep down, they wonder if they should just accept their old life, rather than continue to risk harm.
- **Choice:** If they're to succeed, the rogue will reject this thinking, instead embracing their truth and using it to resolve their story's conflict—thus proving themselves worthy of being treated as an equal, both to themselves and others.
- **The End:** Now secure, the rogue has the power to choose where they go, either staying among their new community or leaving for different horizons. No matter their choice, they do so under their own power, comfortable with who they are and their place in their world.

Basically, what this comes down to is mindset.

The hermit begins their story numb, or at least complacent. They've accepted their isolation from other people, and aren't striving to change that—at least until the events of your story kick their arc into gear. In contrast, the rogue is grasping at straws from the start, desperately trying to gain the security, stability, and safety that comes from being a full member of the human world.

What's really fascinating about these two arcs is just how much they reject the qualities of the classic hero or heroine.

While they can certainly represent traits like kindness, bravery, wisdom, or courage, both the hermit and the rogue are just as likely to be rough, abrasive, desperate, or even cruel. This is why so many anti-heroes fall under one of these secondary arcs—with Han Solo from the original *Star Wars* trilogy being a famous example.

Deep down, these characters might have hearts of gold, but they're covered in so many layers of armor that their heart is often hard to see.

Case Study: Rick Blaine and Sinbad

With that in mind, let's pause to explore these arcs in action.

By now, you know the drill. We'll be looking at two movies for this case study, one for the hermit and one for the rogue:

- *Casablanca* (1942)
- *Sinbad: Legend of the Seven Seas* (2003)

Rick Blaine — The Hermit's Arc

Starting things off, we have *Casablanca,* a romantic drama set in the early 1940s.

This movie follows Rick Blaine, a bitter American expat who runs a bar and gambling den in French-occupied Casablanca. With the Nazis rapidly marching through Europe, this has become a hot spot for refugees fleeing to America, as well as the perfect hunting ground for all kinds of predators and thieves. Despite this, Rick keeps to himself. Though he's frequently asked for help, his motto is, "I stick my neck out for nobody" *(The Beginning).*

This motto becomes hard to abide by after a few key events.

First, Rick is given two letters of transit, which he takes great care to hide. These letters give their bearer safe passage to America, and are highly sought after by those in Casablanca. From there, a woman named Ilsa Lund arrives in Rick's bar, alongside her husband, Victor Lazlo—a prominent Czech resistance leader being hunted by the Nazis. The pair are looking for a way out of Casablanca, and come to Rick for help *(Catalyst)*.

There's just one problem: Ilsa is Rick's past lover, who broke his heart years ago after abandoning him without warning.

Rick is still deeply in love with Ilsa, but has never forgiven her for leaving him behind. Because of this, Rick refuses their request, angry that his isolation has been disturbed *(The Reactive Phase)*. This eventually culminates in an argument between Lazlo and Rick. Though Rick continues to deny any help, he also supports Lazlo in the face of Nazi officers, getting his club shut down in the process *(Turning Point)*. With his normal sanctuary disturbed, he struggles with his decision not to help Ilsa *(The Active Phase)*.

Meanwhile, Ilsa and Lazlo's situation is getting dire. They're running out of time, and so Ilsa goes to Rick in secret. At first, she threatens to shoot him if he doesn't give up the letters, but eventually admits that she still loves him. This offers Rick a chance to take her back, even though he knows it would be wrong—both for him and for her *(Regression)*.

Realizing what he must do, he promises Ilsa that he'll send Lazlo on to America. However, when the pair meet him at the airport, he gives them both letters of transit. He tells Ilsa to stay with her husband, or risk regretting her decision for the rest of her life *(Choice)*. As Ilsa and Lazlo's plane departs, Rick returns to Casablanca, ready to protect his new world *(The End)*. He's forgiven the wounds of his past, and instead embraced the potential his future holds.

Though Rick's wilderness is mostly metaphorical, this story is a perfect example of the hermit's arc at work!

Sinbad — The Rogue's Arc:

From there, we can move on to the rogue's arc, as well as the mischievous Sinbad.

Sinbad is the leader of a crew of pirates, on the hunt for the magical "Book of Peace." This book ensures the safety of the kingdom of Syracuse, and would thus fetch a large price if it was under threat—giving Sinbad the chance to retire once and for all *(The Beginning).*

Of course, Sinbad isn't the only one searching for this book.

While pursuing it, Sinbad falls prey to Eris, the Goddess of Discord. She promises him any reward he desires in exchange for the book, and Sinbad agrees *(Catalyst).* However, while attempting to steal it, Sinbad runs into his childhood friend Proteus. Proteus is charged with protecting the book, and though Sinbad is hurt that he suspects him, he also realizes he can't betray his friend. However, Eris is one step ahead of him. Framing Sinbad for the theft, she takes the book and throws Syracuse into disarray *(The Reactive Phase).*

At this point, everyone believes Sinbad is guilty, and he's sentenced to death for his crimes. However, Proteus stops them. He offers to stand trial on Sinbad's behalf, giving Sinbad a chance to retrieve the book and prove his innocence *(Turning Point).* With the knowledge that his friend will be executed if he doesn't return, Sinbad sets out to find Eris *(The Active Phase).*

Once again, Eris is ready. When Sinbad and his crew finally reach her lair, she offers him a deal: answer her truthfully, and she'll give him the book without question. Sinbad agrees, so she asks him if he would return to Syracuse willingly to face execution or leave his friend to die in his place. He insists he would return, but Eris deems him a liar—thus denying him the book. Deep down, Sinbad can't help but wonder if she's right *(Regression)*.

This is his chance to prove himself.

Though Sinbad knows the consequences will be severe, he makes the choice to return anyway, sacrificing himself for Proteus. In the process, he proves he was honest, and Eris is forced to fulfill her bargain. She returns the book and Sinbad goes free *(Choice)*. Thanks to his actions, Sinbad now has a place in Syracuse, as well as a renewed friendship with Proteus—and though he doesn't stay in this new world, he's safe in the knowledge that he can finally choose his own path without shame *(The End)*.

Lessons from Chapter Nine

Ultimately, if there's one thing I want you to remember from this chapter, it's this:

While the hermit accepts their isolation, the rogue cannot.

This is the real difference between these two arcs, and why these characters feel distinct despite their similarities. Early on, the hermit isn't trying to change their situation. In contrast, the rogue is desperate to. Whether they succeed or fail in this quest depends on you.

In the meantime, here are a few questions to help you apply what you've learned to your cast:

- What is your character's role in society when their arc begins?
- Are they isolated in the wilderness, or are they stuck somewhere along the edge?

- How does this impact their relationships with the people around them?
- What event (or events) could eventually bring your character back into the fold?

Once you've answered these questions, I'll see you in Chapter Ten!

10

LEARNING ABOUT LOVE

If there's one thing I've learned from romance authors, it's that being in love is complex.

From the moment their eyes meet and sparks fly, to the day they finally say "I love you," your characters will be on an emotional roller coaster—and you'll be hard at work too! Beyond the normal challenges of writing an engaging novel, you'll also need to consider all kinds of romantic patterns and pitfalls if you plan to leave your readers swooning.

This isn't limited to romance novels either.

Though there are plenty of romance-specific conventions, the reality is that characters meet, fall in love, and struggle to be together in nearly every genre out there. Love is a big part of the human experience. It's no wonder that it shows up in everything from crime thrillers to fantasy.

So, what should you do? What tools are available to make navigating these budding relationships a little bit easier? Well, his is a book on character arcs, so you can probably guess what I'm about to say...

You need the lover's arc!

Unpacking the Lover's Arc

For the most part, the lover's arc is exactly what it sounds like. This is an arc about learning to balance another person's needs with your own, while also navigating the many dangers of falling in love. Though it might not look like it on the surface, love is a risky thing. Your characters will have to confront a lot of difficult emotions, learn to be vulnerable, and eventually put their trust in their new partner if they have any hope of building a healthy relationship.

With that said, their journey won't start out quite so intense.

The lover's arc begins like most do, with a single spark. In this instance, that spark comes in the form of meeting someone they're attracted to, before growing closer, and eventually realizing they love them. At this point, most characters panic, shying away from this realization and overcome by all the fear it brings. Whatever their inner struggle is, it'll cause them to believe a variety of twisted things about why they and their partner can't be together.

Luckily, these fears don't last forever! Slowly but surely, your lover will come back around, before eventually embracing their partner once and for all.

All of this boils down to three basic steps:

- **Falling in Love:** The lover meets their future partner and—though they'll likely butt heads at first—slowly grows attached to them. This is where the lover first realizes their true feelings.
- **Running from Love:** Afraid of being hurt, the lover will put up their armor, rejecting their partner and

trying to go back to "how things were." This is when their inner struggle is at its height.

- **Returning to Love:** Finally, after much reflection, the lover returns to their partner. Through some active decision, they prove they're ready for a relationship, allowing their new life to start.

What's interesting about this arc is that it's almost the exact opposite of the coming of age arc. In that in arc, your character fights to separate themselves from their guardians, slowly learning to stand on their own before establishing themselves as an independent adult. In contrast, the lover's arc is all about coming together. Here your character must learn to sacrifice parts of their independence in order to balance their needs with those of the person they love—binding them together as a pair.

Of course, this arc still follows all the stages you're used to:

- **The Beginning:** The lover starts out living in their normal world, uneasy due to their inner struggle. While some lovers are already acquainted with their soon-to-be partner at this stage, plenty get their first introduction right before their arc kicks into gear.
- **Catalyst:** This happens at the Catalyst, when the lover is forced together with their partner due to some choice they make. From now on, these two characters won't be able to escape each other—at least until they resolve your core conflict.
- **The Reactive Phase:** Slowly, the pair will start to fall in love, initially based on simple attraction. As they struggle, make mistakes, and get to know each other, this attraction will morph into mutual respect. Each partner will teach the other valuable lessons, even as

they butt heads and refuse to recognize their budding romance.

- **Turning Point:** This builds into the Turning Point, where the lover will accept their partner for the first time. This is closely tied to their truth, and usually manifests as a moment of vulnerability. Whether a passionate sex scene or a deep conversation, this is a sign your pair is beginning to trust each other, and thus embrace their relationship.
- **The Active Phase:** Having acknowledged their romantic feelings, the lover will begin pursuing this new relationship more directly. However, their inner struggle is still dragging them down—while the core conflict of your story starts putting more and more obstacles in their way.
- **Regression:** This leads to a painful defeat, where the lover's relationship will appear to fracture. As far as they can tell, they've failed, both to resolve your plot and care for their partner. In reaction, the lover retreats into their shell, isolating themselves as they struggle to confront their inner struggle.
- **Choice:** Eventually, the lover will embrace their truth, giving them the strength to return to their partner. In doing so, they accept the vulnerability required for a happy relationship, sacrificing some of their old beliefs and desires in order to prove how much they've grown.
- **The End:** Thanks to the decisions they make at the Choice, the lover's relationship flourishes, bringing them and their partner together for the long term.

As you can see, the lover begins their arc when they and their new partner are (often begrudgingly) thrust together. Think of a snowstorm stranding old acquaintances in a remote cabin, or the moment Sandra Bullock bullies Ryan Reynolds into a marriage of convenience in *The Proposal*. Whatever this Catalyst looks like, it's fueled by some decision your lover makes, closely tied to their inner struggle.

THE LOVER'S ARC

The Lover

An arc about balancing our desires with the needs of a romantic partner. To succeed, both lovers will have to earn the other's trust.

Obstacles:

- *Fear of being hurt*
- *The opinions of others*

From there, the two will have to learn to get along.

This is a phase full of mistakes, mishaps, and mayhem, but it ends with the pair slowly growing closer. The more they learn about the other, the more they enjoy their company, and the more their truth comes into focus. This culminates in genuine romantic feelings, which opens up a whole new can of worms.

Can they really be vulnerable enough to accept this person? Can they set aside their own prejudices and goals to make them happy? After all, loving someone requires a lot of trust and compromise—and thus plenty of conflict.

Eventually, the lover's internal struggle will get the best of them, resulting in a moment of failure where they push their partner away. At this point, they'll have to make a choice: either prove they love their partner and are willing to trust them, or let them slip away. If they make the right choice, their arc will end with the pair together, accepting each other's love and finding the happiness they were looking for when their journey first began.

If you have much experience with the romance genre, you'll likely recognize a few key story beats hidden among these phases. Moments like the "Meet Cute" or "The Retreat" are staples of romance novels, and for good reason. Romance readers are some of the savviest shoppers around, and they know what they like—as well as exactly how their favorite novels should unfold.

Despite this, these aren't a strict requirement of this arc.

Though the lover's arc absolutely takes inspiration from the romance genre, it's also designed to apply to a wide range of stories. The lover's arc in this book is broad enough for basically any genre out there, from YA to science fiction, and everything in between. While your lover's arc might be the primary focus of your story, it could also be intertwined with a bank heist, an intergalactic race, or even a dragon hunt. Thanks to this flexibility, this arc works in a variety of places —above and beyond just romance novels!

NOTE: I learned a lot from Gwen Hayes' *Romancing the Beat* while researching this arc. If you are writing in the romance genre, Gwen's book delves into a lot of the specific tropes not present here. I highly recommend it!

Case Study: Peter Warne

For this chapter's case study, we'll be looking at the 1934 romantic comedy, *It Happened One Night*. This movie is widely regarded as one of the best films ever made, and it's also a fantastic example of the lover's arc at work!

Our tale follows a deadbeat news reporter named Peter Warne as he helps a young woman named Ellie Andrews reunite with her fiancé. Ellie is the daughter of the extremely wealthy Alexander Andrew, who has forbidden her from marrying her fiancé on accusations that he's a gold digger. Ellie, however, is having none of it. Spoiled and naïve, she runs away from home on a cross-country journey to New York, where she plans to go ahead with the wedding despite her father's warnings *(The Beginning)*.

Meanwhile, Peter has just gotten word that he's been fired.

Indignant, he buys a bus ticket from Miami to New York, hoping to get his job back. This is where he meets Ellie. Ellie has also bought a ticket to New York, boarding the bus in secret and mistakenly taking his seat in the process. Though he initially yells at her, the pair end up sharing the (much too small) bus seat as they head north *(Catalyst)*.

After a series of wild and often amusing mishaps, Peter eventually discovers Ellie's true identity, and promises to help her reach her fiancé if she agrees to let him claim the money for her story. At first, this is purely out of self-interest, but Peter soon becomes genuinely fond of Ellie. Though he insists he can't tolerate her spoiled attitude, he goes out of his way to help her escape her father's detectives *(The Turning Point)*, has a touching heart-to-heart with her, and eventually comes to a complicated realization:

Peter loves her.

This is obviously a problem, as Ellie is en route to marry another man—though she soon admits that she loves Peter too *(The Active Phase)*. Unsure how to show his feelings are genuine, Peter leaves Ellie at a motel, planning to return that evening with enough money to make a "serious proposal." This backfires, as Ellie believes Peter has abandoned her. Returning home to her father, she gets permission to go through with the wedding, even as her heart tells her not to *(Regression)*.

All of this leads to Ellie's wedding day, when Peter arrives at her father's office. He admits to Andrews that he loves Ellie, but that he won't disrupt her happiness or take the reward money Andrews offers him *(Choice)*. Knowing his daughter is making a mistake, Andrews tells Ellie to call off the wedding. Elated, she ends her engagement, rushing to be with Peter—and that night, the two are happily married *(The End)*.

Their lover's arc is complete!

How to Write Lovable Lovers

Now, it's important to realize that tossing two characters together and calling them "lovers" isn't quite enough to make this arc work.

The lover's arc is unique in that it relies heavily on two people, rather than just one. You can see this in our case study. Though Peter's arc takes center stage, Ellie undergoes her own lover's arc too, and the dynamic between them is undeniably endearing. While only one of the pair might undergo a fully fledged lover's arc, they still need to share a genuine attraction—be that sexual, romantic, or both—with their partner.

So, here a few final tips for making this arc feel real.

Consider Their Sacrifice:

One of the biggest components of the lover's arc is sacrifice.

In order to be together and prove they're ready for a relationship, your lover will need to give something up in order to be with their partner. This doesn't have to be huge, but it should be meaningful to them. Accepting some discomfort or changing their goals will go a long way towards proving their attraction is real, and towards showing that they take this relationship seriously.

You can see this sacrifice at work in our case study. At the end of the film, Peter sacrifices the reward money—his original desire—out of respect for his feelings towards Ellie. In doing so, he proves he's changed as a person, and makes it clear that he's ready to accept Ellie's love.

It's this element of sacrifice that takes this arc from "two random people drooling over each other" to "a genuine relationship worth getting invested in." Though your lovers are welcome to drool all they like (depending on how steamy your story is), you want readers to take their union seriously! By adding some sacrifice, you introduce gravity and consequences to your lover's journey.

Create (Interesting) Conflict:

Of course, like any arc, the lover's arc requires conflict.

For this journey to work, there needs to be some obstacle driving a wedge between your two partners—a wedge they'll only overcome by accepting their truths. For Peter and Ellie, this conflict was mostly personality-based, with Peter mistrusting Ellie because of her background. Meanwhile, in a movie like *Dirty Dancing*, the main conflict is primarily external. Baby and Johnny want to be together, but the people around them work hard to keep them apart.

This comes down to two main types of conflict:

- **Interpersonal Conflicts:** Many lovers are driven apart due to their own fears or lack of trust, as well as conflicts of personality, desire, or identity. This causes disagreements and misunderstandings, which your lover will have to overcome in order to nurture their relationship.
- **External Conflicts:** Meanwhile, lovers will also have to face external conflicts caused by their environment. This could be anything from physical separation due to wars, work, or other forces, as well as active interference from other people. If their society or community disapproves of their love, you can bet that will make their relationship harder.

Typically, most lover's arcs will include both of these conflicts in some form—though they'll often focus on one more heavily than the other.

Either way, this works to your advantage! Rather than having to rely on tired clichés like constant misunderstandings (that usually feel fake), you can use a variety of conflicts to make their arc meaningful. For instance:

- Your lovers might have opposing goals
- Being together could be socially taboo
- One or both might be restricted by pacts, curses, or other commitments

- The two could have a fraught history that makes trusting each other difficult
- Or they might believe something about themselves that makes being together seem impossible

With that said, the risk with the lover's arc is that one of these conflicts goes too far, making it impossible for your characters to realistically get together. Since this is fiction, you do have some leeway here, but the thorn disrupting their relationship shouldn't be insurmountable.

You'll also want to consider your reader's perspective. An argument or disagreement is one thing, but one partner abusing the other is something else entirely. The lover's arc isn't about one character "enduring" the other, meaning both partners will need to meet in the middle for their relationship to feel genuine.

Make Readers Care:

One of the most important things to consider in any arc is your reader. Making your audience care about your cast is the point of character development (and this book), after all!

Because of this, I encourage you to ask yourself how your reader is feeling at different stages of your story. For the lover's arc in particular, readers should be rooting for your characters to get together by halfway through your novel, if not sooner. You want to make it clear how these two people could make each other happy, even if your characters don't see it themselves quite yet—and you definitely don't want readers to be rooting for an entirely separate pairing either!

A lot of this comes down to complementary personalities.

Though most lovers begin their arc at odds, you should still consider how their traits balance each other. For instance, a headstrong character might be balanced by a more practical one, while a weary traveler could see the world through fresh eyes thanks to their partner's childlike enthusiasm. Whatever their quirks are, those personalities should make sense together, and combine into a healthy relationship.

Don't Worry About Genre:

Finally, one of the trickiest aspects of the lover's arc is genre.

Like it or not, this arc and the romance genre are tightly connected. I drew a lot of inspiration from romantic patterns when building this arc, meaning it would be disingenuous for me to claim there's no relationship between the two.

Still, I don't want you to worry about genre when using this arc. Romance novels come with a lot of unique reader expectations—expectations that don't apply to every story. Though the lover's arc can mesh with these, it doesn't have to. Alongside the more traditional positive lover's arc we explored in this chapter, you could also write a negative or even failed lover's arc, each of which will fall outside the norm.

Because of this, the lover's arc from this book is meant to be agnostic.

This journey applies equally, whether you're dealing with a classic trope like enemies-to-lovers or a more unusual pairing, such as an older couple falling back in love after their kids have left the house. Whatever your lover's arc is about, just don't feel constrained by the conventions of the romance genre—unless you're actually writing in that genre!

Lessons from Chapter Ten

In the end, what makes this arc so unique is that it's built around multiple people. You'll rarely find a solo lover's arc, and will almost always need to juggle at least two unique characters—even if one of their journeys takes center stage. While it certainly isn't *impossible* to write a solo lover, it definitely is unusual, and the dual nature of this arc is what gives it a lot of its charm.

You should also know that not all relationships are built on a lover's arc.

Just like a character can have some destiny and not follow a chosen one's arc, a character can be in a romantic relationship and not follow a lover's arc. Some characters are already in a stable relationship when their story begins, and that relationship doesn't change as your novel goes on. Meanwhile, even characters who do fall in love over the course of your story might not qualify. They could be minor side characters, their relationship could happen off screen, or their budding romance could unfold largely without incident.

Ultimately, the lover's arc is just like any other arc, in that it requires time to unfold. This is a character's journey of internal change, meaning—whatever arc they follow—it'll shake up their life for years to come. In the lover's arc, this simply happens in the form of romance.

If all of this applies to your character, then the lover's arc will be waiting for them!

In the meantime, here are a few questions to help you apply what you've learned to your cast:

- Does your character's internal transformation center on their relationship with another person?
- What choice or decision triggers that relationship (or some change in their existing relationship)?

- How does your lover's personality balance the personality of their partner?
- How will they eventually prove that they're ready for love?

Once you've answered these questions, I'll see you in Chapter Eleven!

11

THE THREE OLDER ARCS

Up until now, a lot of the secondary arcs we've studied have been "younger arcs," focused on characters finding their place in society and settling into adult life.

However, not every character will be in this early stage.

Some characters begin their stories having already found their place, secure in positions of power and settling down after the hubbub of their younger days has passed. These are the kinds of characters often overlooked in many stories. On the surface, they just don't seem as exciting and dynamic as the younger, classic hero—and in a world with increasingly persistent distractions, excitement is the name of the game.

This raises an interesting question: Can these characters have arcs of their own?

The Mother, Leader, and Elder

We have a long chapter ahead of us, so I'll cut to the chase—the answer, is a resounding yes!

Though it might not look like it on the surface, these kinds of characters are actually filled with potential, whether they form the backbone of your novel or play a supporting role within your larger cast. This is where you find the mother, leader, and elder. These arcs are an "older" set of arcs, usually focused on adult characters navigating the later phases of their lives. They might be starting a family, going into retirement, or even facing their own death. Because of this, their journey will be about responsibility, power, and acceptance, whether that's of the end of their reign or the legacy they're leaving behind.

THE MOTHER VS. THE LEADER VS. THE ELDER

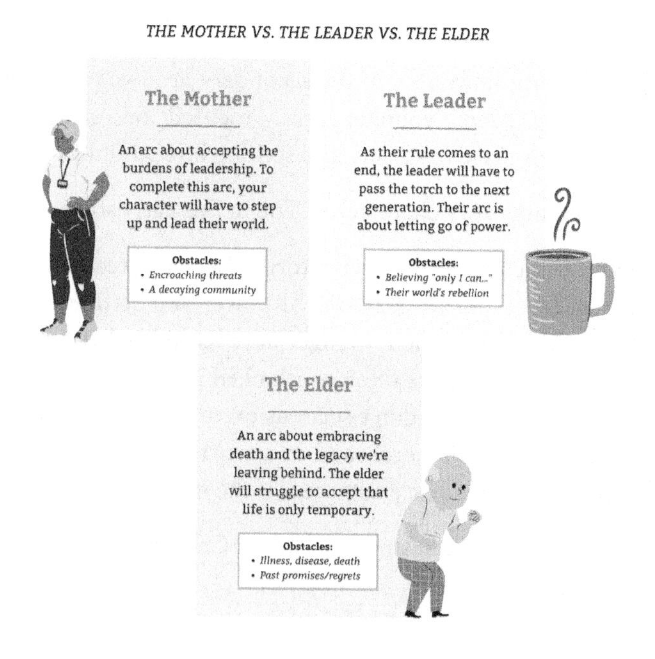

Of course, these arcs aren't limited to only adults—just like the coming of age arc isn't limited to literal children. The mother, leader, and elder's arcs are simply more common in older characters, as they correspond with (at least traditionally) later stages of life.

So, how do each of these arcs play out?

We'll start with the mother's arc.

This is an arc all about accepting the responsibilities of leadership, rising to the occasion and taking on the role of guardian, protector, or parent. This journey is triggered when the mother's community is threatened. Normally, they would rely on their existing leader, but this time something is different—their old leader isn't enough to protect them. Whether their leader dies or is proven ineffective, a power vacuum forms, and the mother steps up to fill it.

In the process, they face deep doubts about their role, before learning to bear the burdens required to protect their people:

- **The Beginning:** The mother begins their story secure beneath the leadership of some other figure, be that a spouse, matriarch, or king. Though they're suffering from some inner struggle and likely feeling discontent, they're unwilling to disturb the peace.
- **Catalyst:** This changes when they realize their old leader can no longer protect them or their community from some growing conflict. The leader's power proves ineffective or misguided, and the mother is called to take over their role.
- **The Reactive Phase:** At first, the mother will be held back by their inner struggle, unwilling to accept the burdens of leadership. Instead, they hope to simply "fill the gap," holding down the fort until their old leader can return or a new leader can be found.
- **Turning Point:** This culminates in a major challenge, where the mother's leadership is tested. Here they'll

embrace their role as guardian for the first time, thus gaining the respect and support of their community.
- **The Active Phase:** Now more comfortable in their role, the mother takes charge, working to resolve the threat to their world. Still, their inner struggle lingers—there are certain risks and sacrifices required of them that they're too afraid to face.
- **Regression:** This comes back to haunt them during a major defeat. The mother is called to accept these risks and refuses, unwilling to endanger themselves or their charges. This leaves their community without a leader, putting their world into jeopardy.
- **Choice:** If they're to succeed, the mother must eventually return, embracing their truth and guiding their community as they face the threat together. They accept the sacrifices required of them and ultimately earn their people's trust.
- **The End:** This journey ends with the mother fully settled into the role of leader, confident in their ability to safeguard the prosperity of their world!

Though it might look like it on the surface, this mother's arc isn't just the chosen one's arc in a different form—though they are often linked.

Chosen one characters frequently take on the responsibilities of leadership as a part of their arc. However, their fate is the main focus of their journey, and coming to terms with that fate is their biggest challenge. In contrast, the mother doesn't need some greater destiny. They simply rise to the occasion as they see the people they care about come under threat. This is all about confidence and trust, following a character as they learn to believe in both themselves and the community they're called to lead.

From there, the leader's arc picks up where the mother's arc leaves off.

This character is already the head of a family, the ruler of a kingdom, or the captain of a crew. Their job is to guide their community and ensure their safety, and that is a job they've always managed to fulfill—at least until now.

Unfortunately, the leader can't be in charge forever.

All leaders eventually step down, and this is the focus of the leader's arc. By the time this arc begins, decay has settled into the leader's world. Unrest is growing, fear is spreading, or disease is threatening their safety. With this threat looming over them, the leader will have to face the reality that their time has come to an end. If they're to overcome the conflict of their story and protect their community, they must sacrifice themselves to preserve their kingdom, thus passing the torch to a new generation.

This makes the leader's arc one of acceptance, following a character as they relinquish power to save their people:

- **The Beginning:** The leader begins their story watching over their community amid prosperity and security. However, a threat is building on the horizon. Though the leader might not fully grasp what that threat is just yet, they dread the day they'll have to face it.
- **Catalyst:** This day arrives with the Catalyst. Some change occurs, meaning the leader can no longer wait to address the problems threatening their people. They must act now, so they make the choice to face this threat head on.
- **The Reactive Phase:** Unfortunately, this proves more complex than they thought, and the leader

soon realizes their plans aren't working. Still, they persist. If they can't solve this conflict, their community is in grave danger.

- **Turning Point:** It's at this point that the leader faces a major test—a test which they appear to fail. Though they're still in charge, their community begins to question their leadership, and even the leader feels doubt creeping in.
- **The Active Phase:** With this failure weighing on them, the leader becomes isolated, focusing all of their energy on solving the threat to their people. For some, this means physically stepping away, while others separate themselves only mentally. However this happens, their community grows concerned about their ability to protect them. Suddenly the leader appears weak in a way they never have before, and mistrust sets in.
- **Regression:** This reaches its peak when the leader is mortally wounded, either literally or figuratively. Their power is gone, and their world is left in disarray. Often, a usurper will take over or a rebellion will occur. Either way, the leader must accept that they alone aren't enough to guide their people. Their time is over.
- **Choice:** Defeated, the leader faces a choice: relinquish power or allow their community to decay. This choice might be literal, with the leader handing power to a chosen successor, while others experience a symbolic choice, accepting the ideas of a new generation and thus breathing life back into their world. Whatever their choice is, they must sacrifice their own desires to safeguard their people.
- **The End:** Finally, if they made the right choice, the leader steps down. The threat has been resolved, and

they're secure in the knowledge that their community is safe once more.

This arc differs from many of the others we've discussed, in that the leader appears to fail on almost all fronts. They rarely get a big moment of "victory," at least until the end of their arc. Instead, the leader is challenged at every turn, either by outside threats, the doubts of their community, or their own fears.

This is a big part of what makes the leader's arc so impactful. Because the leader begins their story already in a position of power, their quest is less about discovering their own abilities and strengths, and more about accepting their weaknesses. After so long in control, it'll take a lot for the leader to recognize their flaws and confront their inner struggle—whether they're a parent watching their child leave home or a queen facing rebellion.

Finally, that brings us to the elder's arc.

This is the last of the three "older" arcs, and is all about accepting the realities of our own mortality and legacy. It's human instinct to cling to life, but to complete this arc, the elder will have to embrace death—not as an enemy, but as a quiet friend. In the process, they'll decide what future they want for their community, work to preserve that future, and eventually sacrifice themselves to ensure the world they leave behind is whole:

- **The Beginning:** The elder begins their story settled into retirement. However, despite the apparent ease of their life, they're discontent or even bitter about the loss of their younger years. At this point, they're simply waiting to die, while their inner struggle prevents them from finding peace.

- **Catalyst:** Soon a threat arises that puts the elder's community in danger, and the elder makes the choice to leave retirement. This may come in the form of a younger character asking for help or a dark warning of some conflict to come.
- **The Reactive Phase:** Back in their old world, the elder struggles with the reality that life has moved on without them. They're no longer as powerful as they used to be, and this apparent weakness fans the flames of their inner struggle.
- **Turning Point:** This changes when the elder faces some major test. Here they accept their truth for the first time, reinvigorating them with the strength and energy they thought they had lost—basically, their "I still got it" moment!
- **The Active Phase:** With a new sense of purpose, the elder strives forward, though they still haven't come to terms with the reality of their eventual death. Instead, they cling to whatever power or status makes them feel alive.
- **Regression:** This culminates in a major defeat, forcing the elder to remember that death is inevitable. As much as they might want to, they can't be there to protect the people they love forever.
- **Choice:** Eventually, the elder must embrace their truth, as well as the world they're leaving behind. In doing so, they sacrifice themselves—either literally or through some symbolic gesture—to save their community, thus resolving the conflict of their story.
- **The End:** Now at peace, the elder is renewed. Here they're resurrected literally or figuratively, allowing

them to live on in the lives of their younger charges. Even after death, their legacy is preserved.

As you can hopefully tell, the real challenge of the elder's arc is twofold. Not only does the elder have to accept their own death, but they also have to trust in their community. This is similar to the leader's arc. In order to leave their world behind, the elder needs to have faith that those who remain can guide it in their stead.

Of course, the elder's arc is often more metaphorical than literal, though some elder characters really do die at the end of their journeys. Either way, this culminates in a symbolic resurrection, showing how the elder's sacrifice allows them to live on despite their death.

An example of this taken literally is Gandalf the Grey from *The Lord of the Rings*. At the end of his elder's arc, he gives up his life to protect the Fellowship, before being revived as Gandalf the White. This resurrection gives him tremendous power, turning him into an almost mythical figure through his acceptance of death.

> "Then darkness took me, and I strayed out of thought and time, and I wandered far on roads that I will not tell... Naked I was sent back—for a brief time, until my task is done."
>
> *THE LORD OF THE RINGS: THE TWO TOWERS*

Last but not least, there is one other variation of the elder's arc that's worth considering.

Though most elders will have to face their own death, some will have to face the death of others. Carl from Pixar's *Up* is a great example of this. Though he's certainly getting on in years, his arc is less about him, and more about the death of his beloved wife Ellie. To complete his arc, he'll have to accept that she's gone and give himself permission to live life without her. In the process, he undergoes all the phases of the elder's arc—even though he himself never dies.

No matter the exact details of your elder's journey, this is an arc all about guidance and mentorship. The elder is almost always paired with a younger arc, if not multiple, and the same holds true for both of the other "older" arcs.

We'll explore those pairs at length later in this book!

Case Study: Maria, Thomas Dunson, and Obi-Wan Kenobi

With those secondary arcs in mind, it's time to turn our attention to three films:

- *The Sound of Music* (1965)
- *Red River* (1948)
- *Star Wars: A New Hope* (1977)

Most of these examples will be based on the positive arc, following the trend of our past case studies. However, there is one exception. Much like the hero and heroine's arcs from Chapter Seven, our case study for the elder's arc will be built on a flat arc.

We'll have an entire chapter dedicated to this blending of primary and secondary arcs later in Part Three, so for now, just keep this difference in mind.

Maria — The Mother's Arc:

First up, we have *The Sound of Music.*

This movie follows a young woman named Maria, studying to become a nun in pre-WWII Austria. Though she's secure under the leadership of the Mother Abbess, she's also discontent. Deep down, she craves the open air of the mountains and the freedom to express herself. Still, she's committed to becoming a nun. Though her truth is the importance of freedom, for her, the safety and security of the abbey are worth the trade *(The Beginning).*

Of course, her unhappiness hasn't gone unnoticed, and so the Mother Abbess sends her to live as a governess in the von Trapp household as a test. Once there, she finds the seven children of the widowed Captain von Trapp, suffocating beneath his strict military discipline. Realizing she can't leave the children to suffer, Maria decides to be an encouraging force in their life *(Catalyst).*

Slowly but surely, her gentle nature earns their trust, though she's careful not to disobey the Captain outright *(The Reactive Phase).* This changes after Maria takes the children to the mountains. They have a wonderful day, singing and playing, only to find the Captain is furious when they return. He intends to punish the children—but this time Maria defies him. She defends their actions, standing up for her truth and earning the Captain's respect by doing so *(Turning Point).*

Now an accepted leader of the household, Maria no longer hides her love for the children. Meanwhile, she and the Captain slowly develop feelings for each other, though she's afraid of what that means *(The Active Phase).* This fear is only magnified when another character reminds her of her training to be a nun. Terrified, Maria flees back to the abbey. Only after consulting with the Mother Abbess does she ultimately find the strength to return home and accept her feelings, thus trading security for freedom *(Regression)*.

All of this happens just as Nazi forces sweep through Austria.

Realizing her new world is under dire threat, Maria devises a plan, sneaking away to the abbey. After inspiring the nuns to help them, the family escapes *(Choice)*. Ultimately, the movie ends with them crossing the Alps to a new life, free and safe *(The End)*. Thanks to Maria's leadership—and the mother's arc that inspired it—their story gets a happy ending!

Thomas Dunson — The Leader's Arc:

Next up we have *Red River,* a 1948 American western that follows the rancher Thomas Dunson as he sets out to complete a seemingly impossible cattle drive from Texas to Missouri.

Dunson begins as the leader of a band of cowboys, as well as one of the largest ranches in Texas. Though he's an unyielding figure, his men respect him and he respects them in return. However, poverty is looming *(The Beginning)*. As his finances grow worse, Dunson decides to drive his herd north to a railroad in Missouri. Though it's a dangerous trip, completing it would allow him to pay his men well into the future. Accompanying him is his adopted son Matt, acting as his loyal advisor *(Catalyst)*.

At first, things go well, but the strain of the difficult terrain takes its toll. The men hear word that there's another railroad in Kansas along a safer route, but Dunson refuses. He has no proof, and won't risk going the wrong way—or losing control of his herd *(The Reactive Phase)*. This comes to a head when one of the men triggers a deadly stampede. Enraged, Dunson intends to whip the perpetrator, until Matt intervenes *(Turning Point).*

Soon after, his men once again ask to take the safer route to Kansas, but this time Dunson kills the men who threaten to leave. The next morning, three others have escaped in the night *(The Active Phase).* When the deserters are retrieved, Dunson orders them hanged. This is a step too far, and Matt takes over the herd, leaving Dunson behind as they divert to Kansas. As a result, Dunson becomes intent on revenge, until he slowly begins to accept that Matt is the son he always wanted *(Regression).*

Eventually, Matt and the cowboys reach the railroad in Kansas. Dunson catches up to them, but rather than kill Matt, he forgives him. Matt has proven himself more than Dunson's equal, and he accepts Matt as their new leader *(Choice).* In a moment of humility, Dunson tells Matt that the ranch is no longer his, but Matt's as well—fulfilling a promise he made at the start of the film *(The End).*

As you can see, Dunson suffers from an inner struggle of control through this story. This inner struggle eats at him, steadily building until the Regression. It's here that he accepts that trust—specifically his trust in Matt—is more important than his own power. He realizes he has faith in Matt to protect everything he's built, and finally comes to terms with the end of his leadership.

This isn't the only trick this movie has up its sleeve either!

What makes this story extra interesting is that it features two of the arcs from this chapter. Alongside Dunson's leader's arc, Matt also undergoes a positive mother's arc, filling the void as the leader of his story descends into decay.

This is a common trend with the leader's arc. Because this arc is about relinquishing power, there needs to be someone waiting in the wings to take over. While far from a requirement, this someone is often a mother's arc, accepting the burdens of leadership right as the leader accepts the end of their reign.

Obi-Wan Kenobi — The Elder's Arc:

Last but not least, we come to Obi-Wan Kenobi from *Star Wars: A New Hope.*

Obi-Wan's story is one you might already be familiar with—but if not, it's a fantastic example of the flat elder's arc! Obi-Wan begins his journey living as a hermit on the planet of Tatooine, looking out for a young Luke Skywalker while hiding from his true identity as a Jedi. Deep down, he already understands his truth of trusting in the Force, but he's also bitter about the failures of his past *(The Beginning).*

All of this changes after the Empire attacks.

When Imperial Stormtroopers kill Luke's family and Obi-Wan receives a plea for help from Princess Leia, he realizes his world in danger. Knowing he has to help, he sets out with Luke to support the rebel cause *(Catalyst).* Of course, the pair needs a ship if they have any hope of reaching Leia's home planet of Alderaan, and so they meet up with Han Solo. Han agrees to transport them aboard his ship, and the group quietly prepares to leave—with Obi-Wan being careful to hide his status as a Jedi *(The Reactive Phase).*

This becomes harder after the Empire is alerted to their position. Under fire from Imperial forces, the group races to board Han's ship, escaping in the nick of time *(Turning Point).* Realizing just how dire their situation is, Obi-Wan begins training Luke in the way of the Jedi. He encourages him to trust in the Force, and Luke slowly accepts this truth *(The Active Phase)*.

All of this culminates in a painful realization—that Alderaan has already been destroyed. When the group arrives where the planet should be, they find nothing but rubble, and Obi-Wan is confronted by the Empire's immense power *(Regression)*. Pulled aboard the Death Star, the group splits up to rescue Princess Leia and find a way to escape.

Meanwhile, Obi-Wan makes a choice.

He knows the group won't get away without a distraction, so he sets out to face Darth Vader, his old pupil and a powerful member of the Empire. Vader represents Obi-Wan's death—and as Luke, Han, and Leia escape, Obi-Wan allows Vader to cut him down *(Choice)*.

Through this, Obi-Wan ends his arc by embracing death and securing the group's safety, becoming one with the Force in the process *(The End)*.

What makes this arc especially interesting is that Obi-Wan's Choice aligns perfectly with Luke Skywalker's Regression. This is a common occurrence in elder's arcs. Since the elder is frequently paired with a hero, their eventual death is often the most painful moment in that hero's story. Though the elder accepts their demise, your other characters don't have to—creating some great opportunities for nuance!

Lessons from Chapter Eleven

Ultimately, a big part of these arcs is how they feed into each other. As the mother grows into a leader, the leader accepts that their reign is over—and, as the leader enters retirement, the elder uses their last days to safeguard their world.

Of course, elders aren't required to undergo a leader's arc, and the same is true for the leader and the mother. Still, it can be helpful to think of these arcs as part of a larger cycle. Human lives are complex, and we'll go through many journeys before our time is up.

Since our characters will reflect our own lives, it stands to reason that they'll have similar, interlocking experiences!

In the meantime, here are a few questions to help you apply what you've learned to your cast:

- Does your character struggle to take on the burdens of leadership throughout their story?
- Are they already in a position of power when their arc begins?
- Will they have to accept their own death to resolve your novel's core conflict?
- Do they have any younger arcs that complement their journey?

Once you've answered these questions, I'll see you in Chapter Twelve!

12

REDEEMING YOUR CHARACTERS

We've all made mistakes in our lives. However, very few of us have made the kinds of mistakes our characters have.

From murder to warmongering and everything in between, many of us write characters who do horrible things over the course of our stories. Even seemingly moral characters can embody negative traits like greed, selfishness, or rage. For enemies and antagonists, this isn't a big deal, because readers aren't meant to identify with those characters. But, what if other members of your cast engage in these harmful acts too? What if they used to be a villain, but you want to transform them into a hero?

Well, that's where the redemption arc comes in.

Redemption arcs are where you take a destructive character and slowly heal them, allowing them to atone for their past actions. Along the way, they'll face a variety of trials, earn key victories, and struggle through painful defeats—just like every other arc we've studied.

Of course, redemption arcs are a bit more complicated than your usual secondary arc. Readers will be looking for any reason to condemn your character, meaning their eventual redemption will be an uphill battle from the start. Fortunately, it also won't be impossible. So, between a few specific elements and some tender love and care, let's explore everything you need to redeem your characters!

Finding the Strength to Forgive

Before we can get into how to write a redemption arc, I first need to answer an important question.

What do I mean by redemption?

A redemption arc is much like any other secondary arc. This is a framework, where a character who starts out evil and destructive—or who embodies destructive traits—atones for their flaws. Through this, they overcome their inner struggle, embrace their truth, and slowly transform from a villain into a hero.

You can see this in how the word "redemption" is defined, as the act of being forgiven for some deep wrong. This is a kind of deliverance or rescue, beyond the normal journey of growth you would find in a typical positive primary arc.

You see, all positive character arcs have some element of redemption. These characters start out flawed and suffering from some harmful belief, before learning how to overcome those flaws and thus find true happiness. So, what's the real difference between a positive character arc and a redemption arc? Well, redemption arcs are simply a more dramatic form of the primary positive arc. A normal positive arc character is flawed, but still on mostly stable moral ground.

In contrast, a character who undergoes a *redemption* arc starts from a much worse place. Their actions are likely awful or borderline unforgivable, meaning they have a lot more work ahead of them to overcome their inner struggle:

- **The Beginning:** Your character starts out flawed and destructive, with their actions harming both themselves and the world around them. As a result, they're shunned or feared by other people. Still, they feel their actions are justified. Thanks to their inner struggle, they don't see how their behavior is wrong.
- **Catalyst:** Eventually, some goal or "carrot" will lure your character out into the world, dragging them into your novel's conflict. They believe this carrot will solve their problems, but it's a false goal—one that represents their inner struggle.
- **The Reactive Phase:** As they pursue this carrot, they'll be confounded at every turn, dragging them farther from their comfort zone. The more they're exposed to new beliefs, the more they begin to question themselves, and the more they strain against their existing relationships and perspective.
- **Turning Point:** This culminates in a major test, where your character embraces their truth for the first time. Through this, they get a taste of acceptance, and are confronted by the reality that their actions are harmful. If they want to turn their life around, they'll need to reject who they used to be and the people that encouraged that behavior.
- **The Active Phase:** Now realizing they're wrong, your character will struggle to change their behavior. However, though they may have some success at first, these efforts will largely be rebuked. They've yet

to address their past actions or overcome their inner struggle, setting them up for failure later on.

- **Regression:** This failure comes at the Regression, where your character will fall back into old habits. In the moment, they'll feel justified, but soon after they'll realize they were deeply wrong. Though it'll be painful, this is their chance to confront who they are and what they've done.
- **Choice:** All of this leads to a moment of redemption, where your character will make some decision that runs counter to their old goals. In doing so, they'll abandon their harmful beliefs, sacrificing something to prove they've changed. This often means their death, but it could also be a symbolic death—one where they defeat a symbol of their past self.
- **The End:** Through this choice, your character will earn the forgiveness of those around them and be redeemed. If they survived the Choice, they'll live at peace within their community, while those that die will be honored with respect.

What sets this journey apart is just how transformative it is.

Don't get me wrong—a normal positive arc character can absolutely require some level of redemption, such as the Beast from Disney's *Beauty and the Beast* or Thor from the Marvel Cinematic Universal. However, whereas those characters learn to be kind and caring to others, they aren't monsters (at least not in spirit). They have mostly positive qualities, and their stories are careful to remind us that they're the good guys, warts and all.

Redemption arcs, on the other hand, begin in a much darker place. These characters start their stories regularly engaging in harmful and destructive behavior, whether as antagonists or a failed heroes. They'll embody negative traits like hatred or aggression—but, they'll also have a weak point. This weak point is some belief, trait, or desire that makes them vulnerable to change, and will thus be the key to their redemption.

THE REDEMPTION ARC

With that foundation established, a successful redemption arc requires two things:

- **Repentance:** First, your character will have to repent for their past actions. This comes in the form of some choice your character makes that proves they've changed.
- **Forgiveness:** Meanwhile, they'll also have to earn forgiveness. To be redeemed, some authority (usually the moral center of their story) will have to accept their transformation and validate their journey.

When combined, these elements work together to create the kind of convincing redemption arcs that win over readers' hearts. Not only has the character themselves embraced the need for positive change, but the people around them have recognized their efforts too. In doing so, you'll slowly coax readers to forgive your character, and hopefully accept that their journey was genuine.

NOTE: Forgiveness is often hard won, meaning your job will be exponentially harder the more destructive your character is—redemption arc or not. Because of this, think carefully about what readers will accept. Some actions are simply to heinous to ignore, even if that character later repents. This is doubly true if your character commits horrible acts "on screen," versus in some nebulous past. Readers will be even less open to their redemption if they've watched them do something unforgivable right on the page.

All of this ties back to your character's weak point.

To spark a realistic transformation, your character will need to experience some key event that breaks their harmful worldview. Whether they hurt someone they love or somehow witness the true effects of their behavior, it's this experience that exploits their weak point, breaking past their armor and thus pushing them to change. This vulnerability is what prevents them from becoming fully "evil," and offers them a chance at redemption.

When combined with true repentance and the forgiveness of others, this creates an interesting secondary arc—and a believable one too!

Slow, Sudden, or Somewhere in Between?

Not every redemption arc requires a long, drawn-out journey. Many stories jump straight to their character's moment of regression, with minimal buildup. Though this is tricky to pull off, it *can* work—and it's where this arc begins to diverge from the other secondary arcs we've studied.

Unlike the coming of age, elder, or heroine's arc, the redemption arc could take one of two forms.

The Slow Growth Redemption Arc:

First up, slow growth journeys make up the majority of successful redemption arcs, and hew closely to the eight-part structure we've already discussed. In these arcs, your character undergoes a complete transformation in full view of your readers. This happens slowly over the course of your novel and is thus the easiest type of redemption arc to write.

Of course, this requires time, which means this style of redemption is usually best suited for members of your core cast. These characters will have plenty of time in the spotlight, and thus ample opportunities to face setbacks, learn important lessons, and slowly transform before your reader's eyes—just like any other character arc.

For example, think of Prince Zuko from the show *Avatar: The Last Airbender*.

We'll actually be returning to Zuko in Chapter Fourteen, but for now, the important thing to know is that he follows a classic slow growth redemption arc. His journey unfolds over three seasons of the show, starting with him as an antagonist and ending as a hero. Along the way, he holds onto his negative beliefs for a long time, and only begins to change after he witnesses the real consequences of his father's war. All of this culminates in multiple episodes dedicated to his struggle to repent. By the time his journey is complete, he's been forgiven by the people around him and successfully completed his arc.

I recommend this style of redemption for most writers.

The Breaking Point Redemption Arc:

Compared to the slow growth style, the breaking point redemption arc takes a slightly different approach—though perhaps not as much as you might think.

In this style of redemption, your character will face a massive test late in their story that spurs them to undergo a dramatic transformation. On the surface, this will appear to be a sudden change of heart, but in reality, they'll have been questioning their beliefs for some time. Unlike the slow growth arc though, this inner turmoil has been hidden from view.

Naturally, this creates a lot of challenges.

To be believable, this style of redemption requires a major sacrifice on the part of your character, often in the form of their death. It's rare for readers to forgive a character whose transformation is so sudden. By killing them off, you make their act of repentance final, and thus minimize the sticky question of whether they really "deserved" to be forgiven.

As a result, the breaking point redemption arc is best suited for secondary characters who spend most of their time off screen—or whose actions have been so reprehensible that only the most severe consequences can redeem them.

For example, consider Darth Vader, specifically his arc in the original *Star Wars* movies. From the very first scene in *A New Hope,* Vader plays a key role as the antagonist of the trilogy. Luckily, he also has a major weak point—that being his love of his son, Luke Skywalker. As his story reaches its end, Vader is forced to make a choice: either watch his son die, or save Luke and betray the Dark Side. He chooses the latter, dying shortly after in his son's arms.

While there are hints at Vader's humanity throughout this trilogy, he doesn't get much overt character development until his final moments. Instead, the stages of his redemption arc happen in the background, coming to fruition in a climactic finale.

At the end of the day, both of these options have their place, though I won't deny that the breaking point redemption arc is much harder to pull off.

Because of this, I recommend leaning towards the slow growth style whenever possible. This gives you more room to explore your character, let them learn and make mistakes, and hopefully win readers over as their journey unfolds. If you think about this like any other arc, it makes sense that a slow, steady transformation is ideal—though the breaking point style is certainly there if you need it.

Lessons from Chapter Twelve

Out of all the secondary arc we've studied, the redemption arc is definitely one of the more complicated ones. Between it, the lover's arc, and the hybrid arc (more on that in the next chapter), you have a lot of complex options to choose from.

For this arc in particular, your biggest challenge will always be your readers. Though *you* might forgive your character, readers are much more stubborn, meaning you'll need to take great care as you craft your character's transformation.

So, before we wrap up, let me leave you with a few final tips for making this arc work:

- Make sure your character has a clear path to redemption early in your story
- Find their weak point, then exploit it often
- Force them to face trials that match the severity of their harmful actions
- Allow them to struggle, and don't make their redemption a simple "three-step program"
- Pay attention to the rest of your cast—they are who will ultimately forgive your character

Combine these tips with everything you've learned in this chapter and readers will have a hard time shutting your character out of their hearts!

In the meantime, here are a few questions to help you apply what you've learned to your cast:

- What destructive belief haunts your character early in their story?
- What helps them realize they need to change?
- How will your character atone for their past actions?
- Will these sacrifices be equal in severity to the wrongs they've committed?
- Who will ultimately forgive your character and complete their redemption?

Once you've answered these questions, I'll see you in Chapter Thirteen!

13

FINDING THEIR PATH

The beauty of character arcs is that they're all about the journey.

Though your character's final transformation is important, what really captures readers' hearts is watching that transformation play out over time. From following your character as they face struggles and obstacles, to cheering them on as they slowly grow, this is what gets readers invested in their adventure. Now, when your finale finally hits, your new fans will be practically glued to the page.

Of course, there's more than one way for these journeys to unfold.

Over the last six chapters, we've been hyper focused on the many types of secondary arcs your characters could follow—but they'll also have a primary arc too. These primary arcs form their foundation, and thus play a major role in determining the shape of their story. If you truly want to understand your character's journey, you'll need to consider both their primary and secondary arc, as well as how those arcs influence each other.

So, with your new suite of secondary arcs in hand, it's time to discuss how those arcs might combine!

Combining Primary and Secondary

As a quick refresher, primary arcs are your character's baseline. These arcs determine the overarching journey they'll go on, as well as the final outcome of their story—whether that story focuses on growth, decay, or healing.

Since it's been a while since we originally discussed these, here's a brief rundown of the three primary arcs:

- **The Positive Arc:** The positive arc is all about growth. Here your character starts out suffering from some inner struggle, faces tests and trials, and ultimately realizes an important truth. It's through this truth that they overcome their inner struggle and resolve the conflict of their story.
- **The Negative Arc:** In contrast, the negative arc focuses on decay. Here your character also starts out suffering from some inner struggle, but rather than overcome it, they succumb to it. They refuse to embrace their truth and thus devolve into a worse version of themselves, leaving them unable to resolve the conflict of their story.
- **The Flat Arc:** Finally, flat arc characters already know their truth when their story begins. Instead, rather than struggling to grow as a person, their arc is about sharing their truth with those who need it—even in the face of great difficulty.

Alongside these primary arcs, your characters could also experience a failed arc, which is what happens when their story ends in limbo. This is a modifier you can apply to any arc you write, from a failed positive arc to a failed flat rogue's arc—more on that one when we get to our case study.

Speaking of the "flat rogue", you'll also have the option of layering on additional secondary arcs.

These are the more specialized, optional arcs we've focused on throughout Part Three, which help you write about common experiences such as coming of age or redemption. When combined with primary arcs, these secondary arcs open up a world of possibilities, as well as tons of interesting combinations for writing vibrant characters!

In total, there are dozens of combos you could choose from. So, let's explore your options in a bit more detail.

The Hero's Arc

Starting things off, we have the hero's arc.

In this arc, your character sets out into the unknown in search of physical mastery over their world. While there, they face their inner struggle and earn some reward, before eventually returning to their known world to share that reward with their community.

Of course, this is only the positive version of this arc. In this version, the hero succeeds in embracing their truth and earning their reward, before making the difficult choice to leave the unknown and return to the known. In contrast, the negative version of this arc takes a darker turn. Here, the hero rejects either their truth or their role as hero, refusing to return home and letting their society to fall into neglect.

Finally, the flat hero's arc operates much like the positive one, with a few key differences. In this version, the hero successfully earns their reward not through their own growth, but by proving their dedication to their truth. With that reward in hand, they return to the known, proving their truth and healing their community in the process.

This means the hero's arc can take one of three forms:

- **The Positive Hero's Arc:** The hero successfully earns their reward by embracing their truth and overcoming their inner struggle, before returning to their known world to share that reward with others.
- **The Negative Hero's Arc:** The hero either fails to accept their truth or refuses to return home after earning their reward. This leads both them and their society to suffer.
- **The Flat Hero's Arc:** The hero earns their reward not through personal growth, but by proving their truth is real, before returning to their known world to heal the wounds of their community.

The Heroine's Arc

Next up, the heroine acts as a mirror of the hero.

Whereas the hero's arc is focused on your character's mastery over their physical world, the heroine's arc is more concerned with their mastery over their own self. This arc follows your character as they set out into the unknown, face difficult trials, and eventually rekindle their understanding of their true identity, desires, and needs. With that deeper wisdom in hand, they then return to their community, restoring balance to their known world by sharing what they've learned with their people.

The negative version of this arc fails somewhere along the way. While the positive heroine successfully embraces their true self, the negative heroine only sinks deeper into their harmful beliefs. They double down on the restrictions of their old identity, cling to their old habits, and eventually self-destruct as a result.

Last but not least, the flat heroine is all about resilience.

This variation follows a heroine who already understands their true self—but who is unable to show it. Perhaps they're afraid of what their identity might mean, or maybe they live in a world that denies who they are. Either way, their story will be about overcoming these barriers, standing up for their truth as they slowly heal the people around them.

This means the heroine's arc can take one of three forms:

- **The Positive Heroine's Arc:** The heroine succeeds in developing a deeper understanding of themselves, before returning to their known world to share their wisdom with others.
- **The Negative Heroine's Arc:** The heroine fails to accept who they are, retreating deeper into their false identities and becoming destructive—both to themselves and others—in the process.
- **The Flat Heroine's Arc:** The heroine slowly learns to stand up for the truth they already know about themselves, giving them the strength they need to bring balance to their community.

The Coming of Age Arc

The coming of age arc is a classic journey, one rooted in the difficult transition from child to adult. In this arc, your character will have to reject their child world, discover their own individual identity, and navigate the many challenges of adulthood. If they succeed, they'll embrace their truth and earn the right to be respected as an adult—but if they fail, they'll be pulled back into their child world.

This is where you'll find the negative coming of age arc.

These characters are those who fail to assert their independence, either returning to their old guardians or succumbing to new and dangerous predators. As a result, they end up trapped. They're unable to pursue their own path, and so they wither away until they're just a shell of their true potential. They can't forget the freedom of the adult world, but they also can't escape their childhood.

Finally, in the flat coming of age arc, your character already knows their truth at the start of their story—but they're unable to live that truth due to their guardians. To remedy this, they'll have to find the strength to stand alone, even as the people around them hold them back. By the end of their journey, they'll have shed the restraints of their child world, allowing them to fully embody their truth.

This means the coming of age arc takes one of three forms:

- **The Positive Coming of Age Arc:** The character successfully establishes their independence, earning the right to remain in the adult world.
- **The Negative Coming of Age Arc:** The character fails to grow beyond their role as a child, either returning to their guardians or succumbing to the control of other characters.
- **The Flat Coming of Age Arc:** The character rejects their child world in order to embody their truth, thus

proving that truth (and their newfound independence) to the world around them.

The Chosen One's Arc

By now, you know how this works, so let's dive right into things.

The chosen one's arc follows a character as they slowly come to terms with their destiny, struggling to reconcile their own desires and identity with what their fate demands. Naturally, the positive chosen one succeeds in this journey. Not only do they accept the responsibilities thrust onto them, but they do so in a way that aligns with the truth they learn throughout their journey.

In contrast, the negative chosen one isn't so lucky. This character either rejects their destiny outright, or becomes so obsessed with it that they lose themselves along the way—à la *Oedipus Rex*. As a result, they can't handle the challenges of their story, and slowly descend into madness or destruction.

Finally, the flat chosen one faces their own struggles. These characters start their stories already knowing their truth, but with a destiny that goes against that truth. For example, their fate might be to become a powerful warlord, while their truth is one of peace. Because of this, their journey is about learning to fulfill their destiny, without betraying what they know is right.

This means the chosen one's arc can take one of three forms:

- **The Positive Chosen One's Arc:** The chosen one successfully faces their fate, accepting the burdens required of them while balancing those burdens with their own needs.

- **The Negative Chosen One's Arc:** The chosen one rejects their destiny, either running from it (in vain) or becoming so obsessed with it that they self-destruct, harming the world around them.
- **The Flat Chosen One's Arc:** The chosen one learns to align their fate with their truth, even though that fate originally seemed at odds with everything they believed.

The Hermit's Arc

Next on our list, the hermit's arc rejects the trend of the classic hero and heroine.

This secondary arc follows a character not as they grow past their society, but as they return to it. Rather than leave their community in search of something more, the hermit must forgive the sins of the past in order to find their place in a world they once rejected. Along the way, they'll relearn both the rules and expectations of this "human world," as well as what they want for their future.

In the positive variation of this arc, this journey is a success. The hermit is coaxed out of the wilderness, slowly forms new, healthy relationships, and eventually heals the wounds that originally drove them away. By the time this transformation is complete, they'll once again be a full, accepted member of their society.

Meanwhile, where the positive hermit succeeds, the negative hermit fails.

This character will refuse to forgive their community or themselves. Depending on what initially drove them into the wilderness, they'll have a lot of pent-up hatred—hatred they simply can't let go. As a result, they'll reject the human world, returning to the wilderness and leaving their community to decay.

Luckily, the flat hermit fares a bit better. These characters are those who abandoned the human world because of their society's unwillingness to accept their truth. However, after years in the wilderness, life has changed. When they finally return to their old community, their efforts will prove successful. Though they'll still face their fair share of trials, their truth will be the perfect remedy for their world's inner struggle.

This means the hermit's arc can take one of three forms:

- **The Positive Hermit's Arc:** The hermit successfully returns to their society, overcoming the wounds of the past and learning to accept their new place in their community.
- **The Negative Hermit's Arc:** The hermit fails to reconcile their past experiences with their new situation, rejecting life outside the wilderness and growing to hate their world or themselves.
- **The Flat Hermit's Arc:** The hermit upholds the truth that originally drove them from society, this time successfully sharing it with the people around them.

The Rogue's Arc

The rogue has a slightly different perspective than the hermit —though these two arcs are closely related.

In this secondary arc, your character will begin their story already connected to their community and a part of the human world. However, that relationship is fragile. The rogue exists on the edges of society, seen as illegitimate and thus denied the support other people might enjoy.

For the positive rogue, this presents the chance to grow. Their journey will be all about finding belonging in a world that rejects them, both by earning their community's respect and learning to accept themselves regardless of what others think. Along the way, they'll be tempted by promises of power and control, allowing them to punish or escape those around them—but, if they're to succeed in their arc, they must reject these opportunities. Instead, they'll embrace their truth, prove themselves a worthy member of their society, and thus gain the legitimacy and security they crave.

Of course, not all rogues survive these tests.

The negative rogue will be unable to let go of their inner struggle or give up on the opportunity to gain power—even as that power forces them to hurt themselves or others. In their eyes, their inner struggle is what keeps them safe, and so they'll double down on those harmful beliefs as they grasp at ways to maintain control. As a result, the negative rogue sells their soul, either literally or figuratively. Rather than embrace the risks needed to forge their own future, they wither away beneath their fears.

This is actually the more common version of this arc, at least in my experience. The rogue's arc is frequently associated with deeply flawed, villainous characters. However, when you step back and view these characters with more empathy, you find they often have no better option. As rogues, their world maligns them at every turn, meaning their only shot at safety is usually through manipulation, even if that manipulation turns them into a villain.

NOTE: If you'd like to see this in action, Qi'ra from *Solo* is a great example of a more sympathetic take on the negative rogue.

Finally, the flat rogue has a gentler journey.

Though this character begins their story trapped on the fringes of the human world, they already know their truth when their journey begins. Because of this, their story is about upholding their truth even as the people around them try to squash it. Eventually, they'll use that truth to change their world's perception of themselves and people like them, thus finding belonging by staying true to themselves.

This means the rogue's arc can take one of three forms:

- **The Positive Rogue's Arc:** The rogue rejects the allure of power or security and instead embraces their truth, thus gaining legitimacy in the eyes of both themselves and their society.
- **The Negative Rogue's Arc:** The rogue clings to the harmful beliefs they believe will keep them safe, doubling down on their need for control and thus sacrificing their chance at freedom.
- **The Flat Rogue's Arc:** The rogue upholds their truth even in the face of ridicule, eventually changing their society's perception of themselves and people like them for the better.

The Lover's Arc

Continuing down our list, the lover's arc is exactly what it sounds like!

This arc is about a character's struggle to accept love, along with the dangers that come with it. From the risk of having their heart broken to the fear of rejection or loss, the lover will have to face a lot of challenges throughout their journey.

The positive lover takes these hurdles in stride. Though they'll stumble along the way, this character manages to embrace the vulnerability required to foster a healthy relationship. In doing so, they meld their needs and desires with those of their new partner. The result is a solid, thriving relationship—not just for the lover, but for their partner too.

The negative lover, on the other hand, isn't so fortunate.

This character proves unable to let go of their inner struggle and trust their partner. As a result, they reject their love, running away and putting up their armor to avoid being vulnerable. Some negative lovers even abuse their lover in an attempt to prevent betrayal. In their eyes, only absolute control can prevent their lover from hurting them, causing them to slowly transform into a monster. Either way, the negative lover destroys any chance they might have had at a happy relationship.

NOTE: Negative lovers are a *very* delicate topic. Abusive romances are no joke and should be handled with the utmost care. If you want to write a negative lover's arc, think carefully about how you portray that character, what your readers' limits are, and what you yourself are comfortable with. Trigger warnings may be wise.

Last but not least, the flat lover's arc is about a character using their truth to lift up their partner. This style of arc is often paired with a corresponding positive lover's arc, creating a story where each arc balances the other. By upholding their truth and supporting their partner—even as the people around them try to tear them down—the flat lover helps them complete their own arc, while also building a loving relationship.

This means the lover's arc can take one of three forms:

- **The Positive Lover's Arc:** The lover accepts that it's ok to be vulnerable in order to nurture their relationship, learning to balance their own needs with the needs of their partner.
- **The Negative Lover's Arc:** The lover is unable to overcome their inner struggle, either rejecting their partner entirely or trying to control them to avoid betrayal—harming them both in the process.
- **The Flat Lover's Arc:** The lover successfully uses their truth to build up and support their partner, even as the people around them try to tear them down.

The Mother's Arc

The mother's arc is about facing the burdens of leadership.

Here, your character begins their story secure beneath the guidance of another figure—at least until that figure proves ineffective. Whether their old leader dies or succumbs to their flaws, the mother will realize they can no longer trust them to protect their community. Instead, the mother will have to take charge, embracing the responsibilities required of them or risking their world falling into disarray.

This leads to a lot of doubt, fear, and resistance.

Being a good leader requires risk and sacrifice, and the positive mother will have to accept these things if they're to succeed. By trusting in their own abilities and in their community's strength, they'll eventually rise to the occasion, guiding their world to safety.

The negative mother, on the other hand, will reject this call to leadership. With their inner struggle dragging them down, they'll be unwilling to risk failure or harm, even as their inaction threatens those they care for. They don't trust themselves or their people to succeed, and so they refuse to take charge, throwing their world into chaos without a leader to guide it.

Lastly, the flat mother's story is one of resilience. As a power vacuum forms, they step forward to take charge, hoping their truth with be enough to guide their people to safety. Though their community will doubt this truth at first, the mother will slowly use their leadership to share their truth with others. By the end of their story, they'll have come to fully embody their truth, teaching those lessons to those who need it most and thus giving them the strength to ensure their world's survival.

This means the mother's arc can take one of three forms:

- **The Positive Mother's Arc:** The mother lets go of their fears and accepts the burdens of leadership, using their new role to guide their community towards prosperity and security.
- **The Negative Mother's Arc:** The mother rejects their role as leader, held back by their inner struggle and thus allowing their world to fall into ruin.
- **The Flat Mother's Arc:** The mother embodies their

truth through their leadership, teaching that truth to others as they give them the tools to thrive.

The Leader's Arc

The leader's arc acts as a continuation of the mother's arc.

Here, your character will start out already in a position of leadership, whether as the ruler of a kingdom, the head of a company, or captain of a crew. However, their time is coming to a close. As the years have worn on, their old powers and ideologies have started to show their age, and they're no longer able to protect their people like they once were. Unrest is growing, and though they'll resist at first, the leader must eventually accept that their reign is over.

In the positive leader's arc, this process proves a success—though not without plenty of mistakes along the way. Fortunately, though the positive leader stumbles throughout their arc, they end their journey by embracing the next generation. They pass the torch, accept the sacrifices required of them, and move on into a well-deserved retirement.

Meanwhile, the negative leader follows the opposite path.

This character refuses to give up power, instead seeking new ways to control their unruly community. When other characters strain against them, they clamp down, becoming increasingly abusive as their hold weakens. Though they may eventually be removed from power, this does not happen willingly—and many negative leaders never give up control at all. Either way, their refusal causes both their world and themselves to unravel and decay.

Finally, the flat leader's arc is perhaps the most complicated of the three. In this variation, the leader clings to power not for their own sake, but because they don't trust their community to follow the right path. They know their truth, but the world around them rejects it. Because of this, their journey is about teaching the next generation, while also learning to reconcile their truth with a changing world. By the time their arc is finished, they'll finally have the peace of mind they need to let new blood take over.

This means the leader's arc can take one of three forms:

- **The Positive Leader's Arc:** The leader successfully passes the torch to the next generation, accepting that their reign has ended and instead embracing the future.
- **The Negative Leader's Arc:** The leader clings to power, becoming increasingly tyrannical the more their community strains against them. As their leadership frays, their world is condemned to suffer.
- **The Flat Leader's Arc:** The leader teaches their truth to the next generation before stepping down, secure in the knowledge that their future is safe.

The Elder's Arc

All of that brings us to the elder's arc, the last of the three older arcs.

This arc finishes the "life cycle" of your character, where they'll be forced to face the reality of their own mortality. Along the way, they'll need to accept their legacy, forgive themselves for the things they never did, and embrace death not as an enemy, but as a friend. In doing so, they'll sacrifice their own life—sometimes literally—in order to ensure the world they're leaving behind can thrive.

Of course, this is only the positive elder's arc.

Alongside this variation, the elder can also follow a negative arc, where they slowly become obsessed with living. This is a classic trope in many old fairytales, where an evil elder sucks the life from younger characters in order to preserve themselves. In the process, they cheat death, finding new and destructive ways to cling to power and thus unleashing horrible consequences.

Finally, the flat elder is much like the flat leader, in that their journey is all about preparing their younger charges to stand on their own. Because of this, the flat elder's arc follows a character as they share their truth with the next generation, before finally sacrificing themselves to secure that generation's future. Though they might fear death, they're safe in the knowledge that their world will be preserved—allowing them to embrace their end.

This means the elder's arc can take one of three forms:

- **The Positive Elder's Arc:** The elder accepts death, sacrificing themselves (either metaphorically or literally) to safeguard their world. In doing so, they transcend death, living on through the legacy they've left behind.
- **The Negative Elder's Arc:** The elder becomes obsessed with living, sucking the life from others into order to preserve their own power and thus triggering dark consequences.
- **The Flat Elder's Arc:** The elder teaches their truth to the younger generation, giving them faith that their world's future is secure and thus allowing them to embrace their death. In the process, they transcend mortality, much like the positive elder's arc.

The Redemption Arc

Last but not least, we come to the redemption arc.

This arc is the odd man out among the other secondary arcs we've studied. You see, while those arcs all have unique paths they could take depending on their primary arc, the redemption arc only has two options:

Success or failure.

Because this arc is all about being redeemed for past wrongs, there aren't the simple positive, negative, or flat variations you'd find in other arcs. Instead, your character will either succeed in earning forgiveness, or fail—either by failing to be forgiven, or failing to repent in the first place. I'd even argue the redemption arc is built on *two* primary arcs in sequence. Your character has suffered through some negative arc in the past, and most now undergo a positive arc in order to redeem themselves. You can't have one without the other.

With that in mind, pay careful attention to your character's journey if you're writing a redemption arc. Though their negative arc can certainly happen prior to the events of your story, they will need both a negative and subsequent positive arc to earn redemption.

Case Study: Eliza Doolittle

It's time to turn our attention to our case study for this chapter—specifically Eliza Doolittle from the (rather complex) movie *My Fair Lady*!

Though there have been many adaptations over the years, for the sake of this case study, we'll be focusing on the 1964 version starring Audrey Hepburn. If you've never seen it before, it follows a poor flower seller named Eliza Doolittle as she's "rescued" from the back alleys of London by the wealthy Professor Higgins. Higgins is a pompous, haughty man, as well as an expert in phonetics. After boasting he could pass Eliza off as duchess just by teaching her to speak properly, a friend dares him to try. Fascinated by the prospect, he takes her on, and Eliza is forcibly transformed into a "proper English lady."

Right away, Eliza makes for an excellent example of the rogue's arc. Because of her poverty, she's relegated to the edges of English society, where other people look down on or outright ignore her. This doesn't change when she's brought on by Higgins. Higgins and his friends treat Eliza like a cheap toy; fun to play games with, but easy to toss aside when they grow bored. Though Eliza slowly makes inroads with some of the people in her life, she's remains an outsider in almost every way.

However, Eliza's primary arc is a bit harder to pin down.

Eliza knows her truth from the start of her story—that being that everyone deserves respect. Yet, she doesn't get the usual closure most flat arc characters enjoy. Though Eliza eventually rejects Higgins cruelty, she finds that his experiment has been too successful. She no longer belongs among her old community on the streets, but is equally out of place in the high-class circles she's been groomed for. Trapped between worlds, she returns to Higgins, rewarding his callous behavior while at the same time holding on to her truth.

This is what makes Eliza a failed flat rogue's arc.

I know, I know—it's enough to make your head spin! Still, you can clearly see the threads of each of Eliza's arcs. Her flat arc is tightly intertwined with her struggle to overcome

Higgins' mockery, while her rogue's arc focuses on her strained relationship with the society she lives in. Both of these arcs end as failed arcs, because Eliza neither heals the inner struggles of her world, nor finds security and belonging on her own terms. Instead, she ends her journey trapped in limbo, showing us one of the many ways these character arcs might combine.

Lessons from Chapter Thirteen

In the end, the best way to approach arcs is in stages.

Choosing a primary arc is typically fairly simple, because each of your options are distinct. Depending on the outcome you want for your character—either growth, decay, or healing—you can quickly see which of the three primary arcs is right for them.

Meanwhile, secondary arcs are more complex. The important thing to consider here is the type of character you're creating, and whether a secondary arc makes sense for them at all. Each of the various secondary arcs aligns closely with classic archetypes like the leader or anti-hero. By thinking carefully about the archetypes your character represents, you can more easily choose from the options available to you.

Of course, you'll also need to consider how their primary and secondary arcs will combine. After all, a positive mother's arc and a flat mother's arc might share the same secondary arc, but their final stories will be wildly different!

This is the real beauty of character arcs.

Though the sheer number of possibilities might feel intimidating now, these combinations open up a ton of room for experimentation. Whatever arcs you gravitate towards, you can rest assured that they'll provide the perfect blueprint for writing a cast of vibrant characters!

In the meantime, here are a few questions to help you apply what you've learned to your cast:

- Which primary arc is the best fit for your character?
- Will they have an additional secondary arc?
- Does their journey end in stasis, or do they get the catharsis they're looking for?
- How do these various arcs combine into a single, cohesive story?

Once you've answered these questions, I'll see you in Chapter Fourteen!

14

THE HYBRID ARC

In the process of researching for *Mastering Character Arcs*, I watched dozens of movies and read just as many books in order to piece together the different types of character arcs out there. It was an exhilarating process, and discovering all the unique journeys our casts could follow triggered quite a few light bulb moments in my own writing life.

However, I also found a lot of oddballs.

For every clear cut lover's arc, heroine's arc, or coming of age arc, there were also stories that seemed to blend all of the above. Some characters went through multiple arcs at the same time, while others hopped from one to another as their lives unfolded. Meanwhile, a few arcs were so tightly woven that I couldn't separate them—doing so would have caused the whole story to collapse.

All of this helped me realize that there was another arc beyond the fourteen I had originally believed—one that blended these possibilities together. So, as we approach the end of Part Three, it's time for me to introduce you to our fifteenth and final arc: the hybrid arc!

Beyond Primary and Secondary

Though it's easy to assume character arcs are strict rulebooks, the truth is that these journeys are only guidelines. Every novel is unique, and the characters that populate them will be unique as well—meaning their arcs could take a variety of unusual turns.

So, how should we handle this? How do these unorthodox journeys fit in our understanding of character arcs?

Well, this is the job of the hybrid arc, which acts as a catchall for the many strange paths your characters could follow. This goes beyond just primary and secondary. Unlike the combinations we discussed in the previous chapter, hybrid arcs are all about mixing and matching multiple character arc combos into one, cohesive journey.

For example, consider a story that follows a character across their life.

Early on, that character might start out as a positive coming of age arc, before transitioning into a failed mother's arc, and later a positive heroine's arc. This is especially common in longer series, where characters have more time to grow and change across multiple journeys. When combined, this means that character will have undergone three complete arcs, woven together into a single adventure.

This is the real purpose of the hybrid arc, which allows you to create multiple interconnected transformations for your characters!

Of course, this makes hybrid arcs somewhat difficult to pin down. Because they invite so much experimentation, they naturally introduce a lot of complex variables—no two hybrid arcs will look quite the same. Fortunately, at least based on my experience, these arcs tend to build around a common two-part structure:

- **A Foundational Arc:** Every hybrid arc will need something to form its foundation. This arc is a single primary/secondary combo that acts as a baseline for the character's story, or at least the majority of their story. Their overarching transformation will be determined by this arc.
- **Extra Supplemental Arcs:** Alongside their foundation, the hybrid arc will also feature a few supplemental primary/secondary arc combos. These are built on top of the foundational arc, and add extra depth to certain parts of their story—though they should always link back to that core foundational arc.

In many ways, this functions similarly to primary and secondary arcs themselves. Your character's primary arc determines their overarching journey (or their foundation), while their secondary arc adds additional, specialized story beats on top of that foundation. Hybrid arcs work in much the same way, just at a slightly larger scope.

Luckily, even though the hybrid arc is more open-ended, that doesn't mean there aren't some common variations to get you inspired! In my research, I found a handful of hybrid arcs that came up again and again, with seven standing out in particular.

Coming of Age —> Hero/Heroine:

The coming of age arc is all about a character rejecting their child world and establishing themselves as an independent adult. Meanwhile, the hero and heroine's arcs are about a character setting out into the unknown, discovering some skill or wisdom, and returning to share that reward with their community.

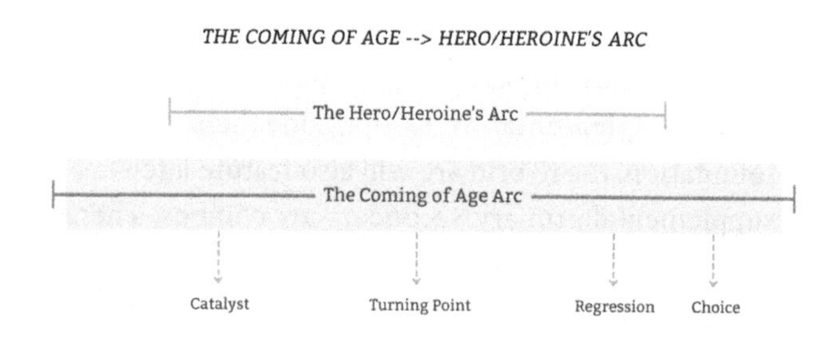

Because these two arcs often target characters in a similar stage of their life, they make great candidates for a hybrid arc combo. This is especially common in genres like YA. As the coming of age character leaves the safety of their guardians, they face the unknown, eventually gaining some reward thanks to their efforts.

Depending on their supplemental arc, this reward could take a few shapes. Some coming of age characters, specifically those aligned with the hero, face mostly physical challenges and thus gain physical rewards. Meanwhile, those aligned with the heroine are more inwardly focused. You can see this by comparing Jim Hawkins from our case study with a character like Rapunzel from Disney's *Tangled.* While Jim's story focuses on his struggle against other characters, Rapunzel's journey is more concerned with her own fears and doubts.

Either way, once your character earns their reward, they'll return home. In doing so, they'll not only complete their "hero's journey," but also establish themselves as an individual worthy of respect.

By the time they earn the title of hero or heroine, they'll have the strength needed to prove they belong in the adult world and thus finish their coming of age arc.

Coming of Age —> Chosen One:

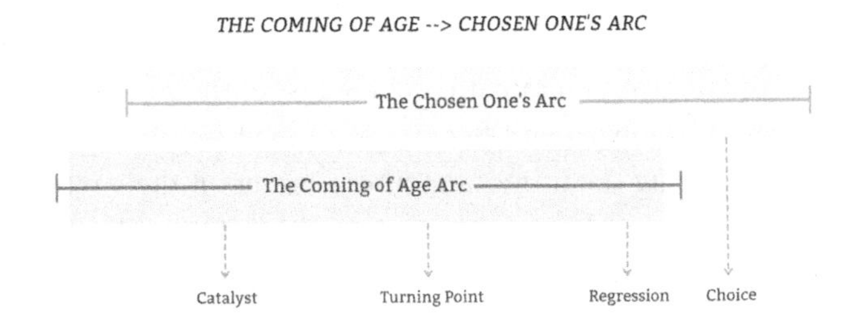

Alongside the hero and heroine, the coming of age arc is also linked to the chosen one.

Again, this arc focuses on a character leaving behind their child world—and what better way to trigger that than with the reveal of some greater destiny!

This reveal is an easy way to jumpstart your character's rejection of the restrictions of childhood, while also forcing them to undergo a concurrent chosen one's arc. By the time they've transformed into an independent adult, they'll also be ready to face the destiny that caused them to grow up in the first place.

Hero/Heroine —> Mother:

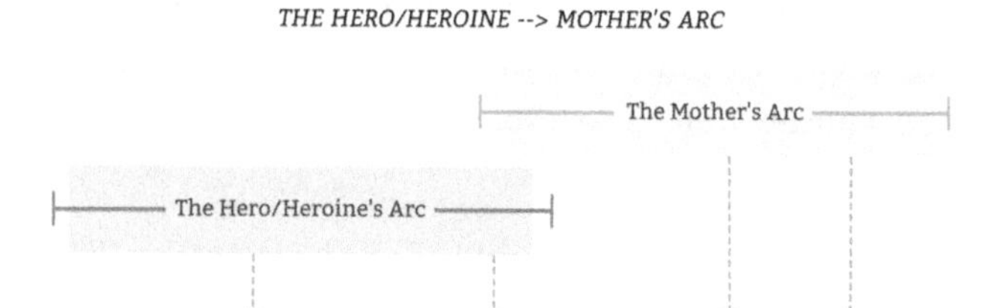

When heroes and heroines return to their known world, they often find their community in disarray.

In the time they've been away, their home has slowly fractured and decayed, culminating in the loss of their old leader. As a result, the hero and heroine are called to take up that mantle, pushing them into a mother's arc upon their return to the known. Just because they've gained the rewards of the unknown world doesn't mean they'll be ready to accept the responsibilities of leadership quite yet—setting the stage for a powerful mother's arc!

Mother —> Leader:

Perhaps the most obvious of these hybrid combinations is the mother and leader.

While the mother's arc is all about rising into positions of leadership, the leader's journey focuses on a character letting go of power. Naturally, these two arcs feed each other. As your character completes their mother's arc and settles into life as a leader, they're setting themselves up to eventually face a subsequent leader's arc as their rule winds down. Usually, this involves a significant time skip, though that's certainly not required.

THE MOTHER --> LEADER'S ARC

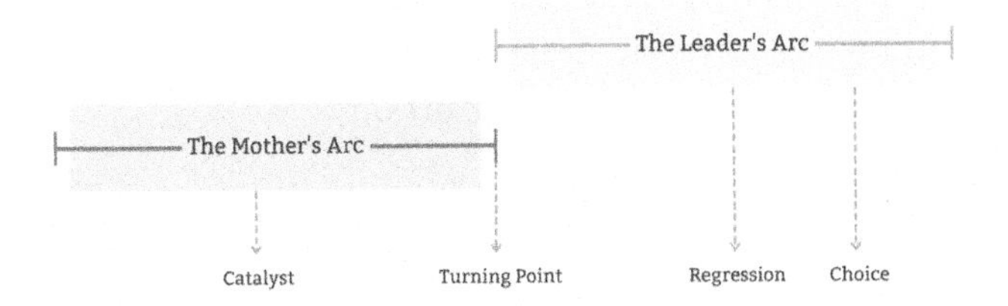

Negative/Failed Hero —> Hermit:

Another common hybrid arc pairing focuses on a twist of the classic hero.

In this variation, your character undergoes a hero (or heroine's) arc, but ultimately fails—either becoming a negative hero or a failed hero. As a result, they never return to their known world, instead remaining behind in the unknown. Eventually, this will morph into the wilderness of the hermit's arc, setting the stage for them to slowly make amends, rediscover their old community, and thus complete their story as a positive hermit.

THE FAILED HERO --> HERMIT'S ARC

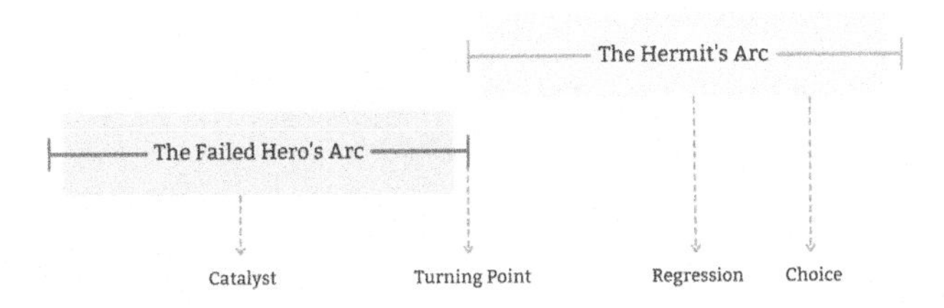

Again, this typically involves some passage of time between the two arcs.

Hermit/Rogue —> Lover:

"Love conquers all" is a common theme in many stories, from romance novels to dramas and even thrillers—and this theme is often reflected in hybrid arcs.

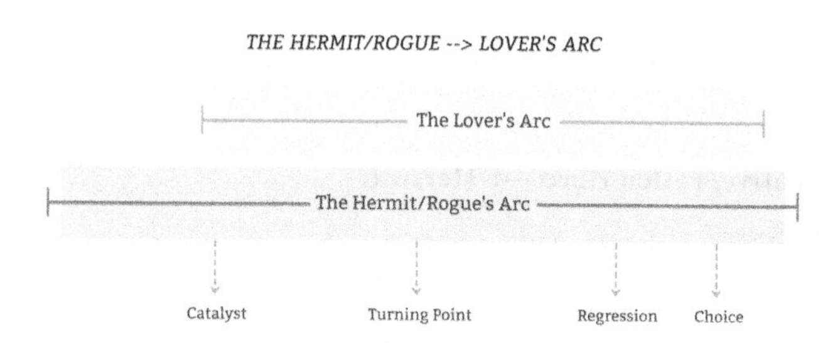

Specifically, the hermit and rogue's arcs often unfold alongside a concurrent lover's arc. As the hermit slowly finds their place within society, they're coaxed out of their shell by a romantic partner, who encourages them to embrace both their human world and their new relationship. Meanwhile, the rogue follows a similar path. As the rogue fights to find safety and security, they also learn to trust their new partner, completing a lover's arc as part of their larger journey.

Rogue —> Mother:

Finally, the rogue faces a lot of unique challenges, challenges that often lead to fascinating hybrid arcs.

One combo I find particularly interesting is the rogue and the mother. Though many rogues learn to live among "polite society" as part of their arc, some reject these groups, instead finding belonging among the downtrodden. In doing so, these rogues are often called to take on positions of leadership, guiding and protecting their new vulnerable community as they face some threat. Through this, the rogue ends up adopting a mother's arc, taking on the role of leader while also proving themselves worthy of being treated as an equal.

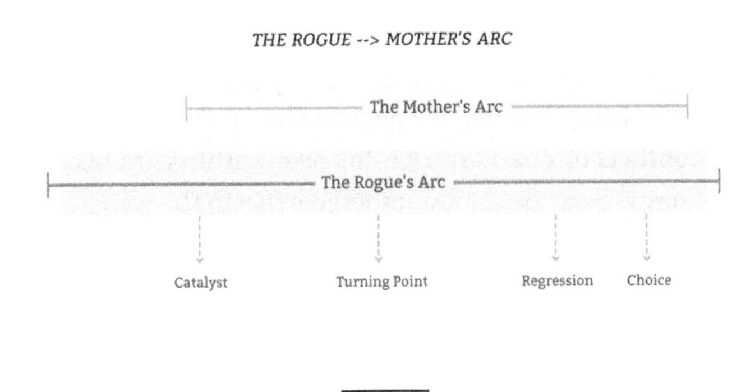

While these are far from the only options out there, this should give you a good idea of how these hybrid journeys might unfold!

Case Study: Prince Zuko

Now that you understand the basics of the hybrid arc, let's pause for a moment to study this arc in practice.

For this chapter's case study, we'll be focusing on the TV series *Avatar: The Last Airbender*—specifically its villain-turned-hero Prince Zuko. On the surface, Zuko is an excellent example of the redemption arc. He begins his story acting as an antagonist, furthering his father's brutal war as he hunts to capture the Avatar, the only one capable of bringing peace. However, he soon realizes his path was wrong. As he travels the world, he sees the pain his nation has caused, culminating in him switching sides and working to end the war. In doing so, he repents for his actions, eventually earning forgiveness and finishing his story as a hero.

Of course, this chapter is focused on the hybrid arc, meaning redemption isn't the only side to Zuko's story! Alongside this redemption arc, he also undergoes three supplemental arcs:

- **A Positive Coming of Age Arc:** One of the major conflicts of Zuko's story is his relationship with his family. Early on, he's smothered beneath the weight of his child world and unable to overcome the hold his family has over him. As he realizes just how wrong his family is, he begins to distance himself from them, establishing himself as an independent person before finally rejecting their control.
- **A Positive Rogue's Arc:** Alongside this coming of age arc, Zuko also goes through a rogue's arc. At the start of his story, he's an outcast, the unwanted prince of his nation. Desperate to change this, he works hard to please his father and regain legitimacy —at least until he accepts his truth. In doing so, he rejects his father's abuse and instead finds legitimacy on his own terms, building a new family out of the friends that support him.
- **A Positive Chosen One's Arc:** Finally, Zuko's fate from birth is to lead his country as his father's heir. Fortunately, he lives up to this destiny, though not the way his father expects. Though Zuko initially runs from his fate, he eventually returns, overthrowing his father and steering his people towards peace and prosperity.

What makes this hybrid arc work so well is that all three of Zuko's supplemental arcs play a role in his redemption arc.

Each of these journeys teach him crucial lessons that tie back into the overarching truth of his story—that being that our worth comes from within. Meanwhile, they also focus on the same (or similar) inner struggle. By completing these supplemental arcs, Zuko gains the strength needed to overcome his harmful beliefs, and thus transform for the better.

Something to keep in mind is that this happens across sixty-one episodes.

Between all three seasons of the show, audiences have plenty of time to get to know Zuko, watch his arc unfold, and piece together the many complex sides of his journey. If you tried to condense this hybrid arc into a shorter run-time, it simply wouldn't work—which is why Zuko is a great example of the slow growth redemption arc too. Zuko's transformation is a success primarily because the writers gave it time to breathe!

The Problems With Hybrid Arcs

Though the hybrid arc is a fascinating one, it also comes with the most pitfalls of any character arc we've studied—meaning many attempts at the hybrid arc just don't work.

Often, authors will try to write a hybrid arc, only to end up with multiple disjointed journeys that cannibalize each other. Without some clear connection between them, none of these arcs reach a satisfying conclusion, and the result is a messy character without a unified transformation. This is why I described the hybrid arc as a foundational arc with a few supplemental arcs built on top. By building outward from a single, central arc, you're more likely to avoid the problems that can arise if you don't have a strong focus for your character.

Here are a few other tips for writing a hybrid arc:

- **Focus on Your Foundation:** Before you do anything else, nail your foundation! The better you understand your character's foundational arc, the easier it'll be to add supplemental arcs later.
- **Write in Cycles:** One of the coolest things about hybrid arcs is that they frequently work like a life cycle. As your character progresses through their foundational arc, they'll trigger smaller supplemental arcs in the process. By thinking of hybrid arcs in these terms, it's easier to see how your character's journey might unfold.
- **Think of Your Plot:** No matter what type of hybrid arc you're writing, it needs to follow the same rules as any other arc. Make sure your character has a clear inner struggle, truth, and story goal, and that their journey connects back to your novel's core conflict, plot, and theme.
- **Weave Them Together:** Try to pick arcs that complement each other! Whenever a major event happens in your character's supplemental arcs, their foundational arc will change too, and vice versa. Because of this, their arcs should always tie together into one, cohesive transformation.

Finally, one of the most important things to consider when planning a hybrid arc is *space*.

You'll need plenty of time to craft these complex journeys, meaning this style of arc is rarely suited to standalone novels —and definitely not to minor side characters. Though you're welcome to give it a try, generally, the hybrid arc is best for major characters like your protagonist or key allies. Combine that with the space a longer series provides, and you'll be much more likely to do this arc justice.

Lessons from Chapter Fourteen

In the end, the human experience is complex, and many of the best stories reflect that complexity. This is the real value of the hybrid arc, much like the failed arc we discussed back in Chapter Six. By having this framework in place, it'll be much easier to understand how these journeys unfold, and how you can recreate them in your own novels.

However, I don't want you to feel like you *have* to use this hybrid arc.

Though this arc is a great option to keep in your back pocket, it's also far more difficult to do justice—and can quickly muddy the waters. If you are interested in writing a hybrid arc, do so with care. Assess all your options and then pick the path that's best for your novel. There's no shame in keeping things simple, so long as the choices you make fit the story you're trying to tell!

In the meantime, here are a few questions to help you apply what you've learned to your cast:

- Does your character undergo multiple connected transformations?
- How do these transformations affect each other?
- Which of these arcs act as their foundational arc?
- What about their supplemental arcs?

Once you've answered these questions, I'll see you in Chapter Fifteen!

IV

BRINGING YOUR CAST TO LIFE

"Don't adventures ever have an end? I suppose not. Someone else always has to carry on the story."

J.R.R. TOLKIEN, ENGLISH AUTHOR AND ACADEMIC

15

FIVE SUPPORTING ARCHETYPES

"It takes a village to raise a child."

Though this proverb might be a common saying among new parents, it's equally true for us as writers. Our characters don't exist in a vacuum. From their childhood best friend to their arch nemesis, kind neighbor, or loyal dog, your characters will be shaped and molded by a wide variety of outside forces.

Because of this, it's finally time to shift our attention to your supporting cast.

Up until now, we've been focusing on just one character at a time, but your novel will likely include dozens of characters (if not more) by the time it's finished. Fleshing out this cast is an important step, but not always an easy one. Though you likely have some ideas for who might populate your character's world, nailing down exactly who these characters will be, the arcs they'll follow, and their role in your novel requires careful thought and lots of practice.

Enter, universal archetypes!

These archetypes provide inspiration and guidance as you build your supporting cast, helping you ensure everyone is accounted for. In any given story, you'll need to balance a range of side characters—everything from more generic "mentors" to specific allies and villains based on your unique novel. When combined, these archetypes lay the groundwork for a compelling story, and pave the way for your character's eventual transformation.

In Part Four, we'll be exploring a lot of tips for building your cast—but for now, let's start with these universal archetypes.

What Are Universal Archetypes?

If you've never heard this term before, archetypes are common patterns and traits writers can use to flesh out their cast—kind of like character arcs themselves. Unlike character arcs though, archetypes are more about the specific role your characters play. They might be a mentor or an ally, or perhaps they're a herald of things to come.

Whatever they are, these roles are *universal,* meaning they aren't the same as genre-specific tropes. Unlike the damsel in distress or knight in shining armor from fairy tales, universal archetypes can apply to a wide range of stories, and thus a whole variety of characters and genres.

For this book, we'll be focusing on five archetypes.

The Mentor:

Acting as your character's main guide, the mentor comes in many forms, from elderly wise women to strict coaches. This mentor is there to equip your character with the knowledge, confidence, and skills they need to complete their arc—though they could also lead your character astray by sharing the wrong advice.

The Ally:

Allies appear in nearly every story, and for good reason. This archetype is who will lighten the load throughout your character's journey, cheer for them when they need it most, and provide support in their darkest moments.

The ally can also be a source of conflict. Saving a companion from danger or earning back their trust are common story beats for a reason—while being betrayed by a once-close friend is a classic plot twist.

The Shadow:

The shadow is closely linked with your antagonist. This archetype seeks the antithesis of your character's goals, as well as the destruction of what they wish to preserve. Because of this, the shadow embodies your character's inner struggle in its worst form, making them the perfect way to highlight the consequences of failure.

The Herald:

This archetype is there to trigger your character's arc, warning of the Catalyst that will eventually upend their life. They might deliver a notice of war, arrive back in town after decades away, or enlist your character's help in a massive heist. Regardless of the specifics, this character "heralds" the changes about to occur.

The Threshold Guardian:

Finally, threshold guardians test your character as they progress along their arc. If your character can't prove they've grown and changed, these guardians will prevent them from moving closer to their goals. For instance, a professor might threaten to flunk your character if they can't pass their midterms, while a prince's father might refuse to crown him king until he overcomes a major test.

All five of these archetypes can trace their origins back to Joseph Campbell's Hero's Journey, which you might recognize from our earlier chapter on the hero and heroine's arcs. Much like that arc, Campbell believed these archetypes were critical to successful storytelling, and I'm inclined to agree. Because each of these five have such a major role to play in your characters' arcs, your cast can't complete their journeys without at least most of them present.

With that said, I do think it's important to understand exactly how these patterns could manifest in your novel. On the surface, it might seem like each of these archetypes needs to be represented by a single, physical character. However, characters can actually embody multiple archetypes, and even non-human forces can play an archetypal role. Many mentors are spirits, ghosts, or figments of your character's mind, while shadows could be anything from massive storms to great white whales!

Either way, all of these archetypes have a role to play in your supporting cast—though what that role looks like will depend on their arc.

Archetypes and character arcs have an interesting relationship. Because your character's arc will determine so much about their unique journey, it'll also play a major role in shaping the supporting characters around them. Though they play the same archetypal role, the mentor for a hero or heroine likely won't be the same as for a mother or leader, because their stories focus on different things.

This is extra apparent when it comes to secondary arcs. The three primary arcs are fairly general, and are mostly concerned with the overarching trajectory of your character's story. In contrast, secondary arcs are specialized. These arcs are full of key story beats and conflicts and thus are the perfect place to find wild and wacky variations on these archetypes—ones that show up again and again across all kinds of stories and genres.

For the rest of this chapter, we'll explore those variations.

Each secondary arc we've discussed will have its own section, complete with a list of the supporting characters that feature in that arc. None of these archetypes are a requirement, but I do hope they get you thinking about the possibilities. While all of these variations share some common DNA with the basic archetypes we just discussed, they open a whole new world of unique characters and personalities. If you've ever struggled to flesh out your larger cast, this is an excellent place to get started!

NOTE: A lot of these terms are associated with the protagonist, but that doesn't mean the rest of your cast won't be affected by archetypes too. Any character with an arc will have mentors, allies, and shadows of their own. The difference will simply be your focus. While your protagonist's supporting cast will likely take center stage, smaller side characters can still have important relationships of their own.

The Hero's Arc

The hero's arc is about a character facing the unknown in search of some reward. Along the way, they'll face a variety of tests and trials, before eventually gaining physical mastery over their world—meaning the hero's supporting archetypes are pretty traditional:

- **The Wise Man (Mentor):** The classic image of the mentor. Think of grizzled wizards and witches, respected shamans, and others who have important wisdom to share with the hero. This character's job is to provide the knowledge, skills, and tools needed to prepare the hero for the unknown world.
- **Childhood Friends (Ally):** Often, heroes are accompanied on their quest by a childhood friend. This character will fulfill all the usual roles of an ally, while also giving the hero a direct link back to their known world. This childhood friend represents home, meaning they'll be a lifeline that pulls the hero back when it's time for them to return.
- **The Benevolent King (Ally):** Alongside a childhood friend, the hero will often be supported by an older leader. This character gives resources and legitimacy to the hero's quest, and is often the one who sends the hero into the unknown in the first place.
- **The General (Shadow):** The general can take many forms, but whoever they are, they are a dark force threatening the hero's community. Typically, they'll be a powerful insider within the hero's known world, or perhaps a cunning outsider seeking to destroy it. Either way, they are a symbol of the disease settling into the hero's society.
- **The Dragon (Shadow):** Of course, the general is only

human—whereas the dragon is something more. This shadow represents some greater force of nature that controls the unknown world and that the hero will have to overcome if they're to survive. While the general's domain is focused on the known, the dragon is rooted in the unknown.

- **The Postman (Herald):** For the hero, their herald is often very literal. The postman is a character who brings warnings of the threat looming over the hero's community, usually through physical messages, letters, draft notices, and the like.
- **The Spectre of Death (Herald):** In contrast to the postman, the spectre of death is more metaphorical. Often this won't be a character at all, but some rot spreading through the hero's community. This represents the cracks in their society, warning your hero that their adventure is necessary to bring their known world back into balance.
- **Ancient Spirits (Threshold Guardian):** The threshold guardians of the hero's arc are almost always a symbol of the status quo—both good and bad. In the case of the ancient spirits, these characters represent the strengths of the past. In order for the hero to continue their quest, these spirits must be satisfied that the hero respects their hard-earned wisdom, preparing them to face the ordeals of the unknown world.
- **The Lost Hero (Threshold Guardian):** Finally, the lost hero embodies the mistakes of the past. This character was once a hero themselves, but gave in to the disease and flaws of your character's current known world. Now, the lost hero intends to stop your character, afraid they'll make the same mistakes

—forcing your character to prove they're wiser than their ancestors.

The Heroine's Arc

Following from the hero, we have the heroine.

The heroine's arc is a unique case, at least in this chapter. Because the hero and heroine act as mirror images, the heroine doesn't have a set of supporting archetypes all their own. Instead, the heroine's archetypes are the same as the hero's, just with a more inward focus.

For instance, the wise man from the hero's arc often manifests as a spirit or other ethereal figure in the heroine's arc. This is because the heroine's quest is about developing a deeper understanding of their true self, meaning a physical character often won't be enough to guide them to this connection. Instead, a ghost or other similar force is able to tap into the deeper, more spiritual aspects of the heroine's arc—though they follow the same basic patterns as the wise man of the hero's arc.

The Coming of Age Arc

Moving on to a secondary arc that *does* have its own unique archetypes, we come to the coming of age arc.

This arc is all about a character achieving independence and establishing themselves in the adult world. As a result, the coming of age arc features a variety of powerful mentors and guardians—character who can guide and test your character as they find their footing:

- **The Wild Child (Mentor):** First up, the wild child is

responsible for encouraging your character to shed the restrictions of their childhood. On the surface, their outbursts seem mischievous or irresponsible, but they play a critical role in teaching your character how to push the limits and discover all the possibilities available to them in the adult world.

- **Big Sister (Mentor):** Compared to the wild child, the big sister is more practical. This mentor teaches your character to respect the responsibilities that come with being an adult, often warning them of the dangers they might experience as they leave the nest. The big sibling plays an important role in balancing the energy and unpredictability of the wild child.
- **A Loyal Pet (Ally):** Unfortunately, the coming of age character is usually supported by few if any allies. Because they're facing such a dramatic shift in their life, a loyal pet is often the only one they can trust. This character represents stability at a time when even your character's childhood friends might be leaving them behind.
- **The Predator (Shadow):** The shadows of the coming of age arc are focused on submission. In the case of the predator, this is a shadow who seeks to possess your character, either through marriage, employment, or some other means. They're uninterested in your character's true desires and instead want to control them in order to gain a new toy for themselves. Because of this, they represent the very real dangers of the adult world.
- **The Parents (Shadow):** Meanwhile, the parents are exactly what they sound like. These shadows are the guardians of your character's child world, seeking to bring them back into the fold. Often, these guardians mean well, but the result is still the same. If your

character returns to the child world, they'll wilt and suffocate, meaning the parents represent just as much of a threat as the predator.
- **Unwanted Suitors (Herald):** Though their name might imply marriage, this herald isn't strictly romantic. Whether a literal suitor or a sports recruiter, draft officer, or debt collector, this is someone seeking something from your character. Through their arrival, they signal that your character has been noticed by the adult world, and has thus become of interest to those in who rule it.
- **The Witch (Threshold Guardian):** The witch is an interesting guardian, in that they often appear to be a mentor—at least on the surface. The witch's job is to put road blocks (often disguised as aids) in your character's path, forcing them to wise up to the realities of the adult world. In doing so, they test your character, only providing true help once they believe they've grown past the naïve child they started as.
- **The Judge (Threshold Guardian):** Last but not least, the judge is someone responsible for either rejecting or accepting your character's place in the adult world. They hold a position of authority, meaning—if they deem your character worthy—others in the adult world will as well.

The Chosen One's Arc

The chosen one's arc is about a character facing their destiny and the responsibilities that come with it. In the process, they'll have to withstand a lot of pressure from other people:

- **A Past Life (Mentor):** Often a spirit or ghost, the past life guides and encourages your character. This mentor has faced this destiny before, and is therefore critical to helping the chosen one master their new abilities and understand what their fate requires of them.

- **The Ascetic (Mentor/Threshold Guardian):** Meanwhile, the ascetic is similar to the past life, but holds a more physical place in the chosen one's world. This character deeply believes in the chosen one's prophecy, and is thus determined to teach them how to fulfill their duty. However, not all chosen ones can live up to the ascetic's high expectations. Because of this, the ascetic often morphs into a threshold guardian, preventing the chosen one from progressing until they're satisfied with their skills.
- **The Congregation (Ally):** Chosen ones often come with a wide cast of allies who believe in and thus validate your character's potential. These allies will stick up for them when their destiny is challenged, and often provide support as they struggle to adapt to their new responsibilities.
- **The Convert (Ally/Threshold Guardian):** Much like the congregation, the convert is a specific character who starts out at odds with the chosen one. They *don't* believe in destiny and thus reject their fate. Slowly but surely, the chosen one will win them over, until eventually they become your character's staunchest ally.
- **The Usurper (Shadow):** As a more extreme version of the convert, the usurper is someone who also denies the chosen one's destiny, but who seeks their power for themselves. This shadow will work hard to remove the chosen one from the picture, opening the

door for them to fill that role—often in a brash rejection of their own fate.

- **An Old Evil (Shadow):** Alongside the usurper, some old evil will haunt the chosen one. This is usually the powerful force the chosen one is destined to face—though not guaranteed to overcome.
- **The Shaman (Herald):** The shaman delivers news of the chosen one's fate. Often, these shamans are respected members of the community, but they could also be an enemy of the chosen one, meaning their prophecies could be seen as a curse.
- **A Rival King (Threshold Guardian):** The chosen one will often be obstructed by a rival king. This character holds a position of power, meaning their help could mean wonders for the chosen one's quest. However, the rival king doesn't trust the chosen one at first. If the chosen one wants to earn the rival king's allegiance and thus the support of their kingdom, they'll need to prove they can be trusted to use their destiny for good.
- **The Groupie (Threshold Guardian):** Finally, the groupie is someone who *adores* the chosen one—maybe a little too much. This character expects a lot of them, but their image of the chosen one is usually unrealistic. Because of this, the groupie often inflates the chosen one's ego, causing them to struggle when they realize they aren't living up to the groupie's expectations.

The Hermit's Arc

Next up, we have the hermit's arc, my favorite of the twelve secondary arcs!

Rather than follow a character as they set out into the unknown, the hermit's story is all about returning to society. They've been living in the wilderness for some time, and now must make the difficult journey back to their "human world." This sets the stage for a complex collection of supporting archetypes—and a dire shortage of mentors:

- **An Old Friend (Ally):** Though the hermit may have been isolated for many years at the start of their story, they often reunite with an old friend upon their return to the human world. This character is one of the trusted few who managed to stay connected to the hermit throughout their time in the wilderness, and who will play a big role in supporting the hermit as they adjust to their new situation.
- **A Witness (Ally/Mentor):** One of the biggest challenges facing the hermit will be the opinions of other people. Because they start their story as an outsider, it makes sense that some will be suspicious of them. The witness serves to assuage those fears. This character sees the hermit for who they are and vouches for them to the rest of their community. Many witnesses also act as a mentor. Because of their isolation, hermits often lack a strong mentor figure, leaving the witness as the only one to guide them as they find their footing.
- **The Brand (Shadow):** Something originally drove the hermit away from their society, and that something is (or is represented by) the brand. This shadow is a symbol of the hermit's old wounds, and haunts them from the moment they reenter the human world. In order to complete their arc, they'll have to forgive or otherwise overcome this reminder.

- **The Twisted Sibling (Shadow):** The twisted sibling, meanwhile, is a more traditional antagonist. They act as a foil of the hermit, forcing the hermit to face a manifestation of the exact flaws they're running from. You can think of the twisted sibling as a younger brother who emulates the worst traits of their elder brother, becoming a menace in the process.
- **The Bridge (Herald):** Just like something drove the hermit away, something will also need to coax them back. That is the bridge, who pulls the hermit out of the wilderness during their Catalyst. Often, this character comes to the hermit for help, but other times they simply cause the hermit to realize there's something worth returning for.
- **The Town Mayor (Threshold Guardian):** The town mayor is a symbol of the hermit's old community, holding a position of leadership and respect in the human world. This means they hold the keys to the hermit's acceptance, forcing the hermit to prove they belong before the mayor supports them. Usually, the witness will play a major role in swaying the town mayor's opinion.
- **The Innocent (Threshold Guardian):** Finally, the innocent acts much like the town mayor, but in reverse. This is someone who is powerless in their community and thus vulnerable to harm. Through this character, the hermit will show their true colors, either helping or hurting them. Depending on their response, other characters (and your readers) will judge them appropriately.

The Rogue's Arc

A close cousin of the hermit's, the rogue's arc follows a character who exists on the fringes of their society, and who must struggle to find their footing despite that. This doesn't lend itself to many supportive mentors—again, much like the hermit. Instead, the rogue's journey is full of shadows, along with a few returning faces from the hermit's arc:

- **Street Rats (Ally):** One of the rogue's few allies will be other outcasts like them. These street rats are some of the weakest members of the rogue's society —but in return, they're fiercely protective of their own. Because the rogue shares many of their experiences, they'll treat the street rats with respect, and earn themselves a helping hand in return.
- **The Witness (Ally/Mentor):** Returning from the hermit, the witness serves to vouch for the rogue as they struggle to gain legitimacy within their community. This character fills the same role here (both ally and mentor) as they did in the hermit's arc.
- **The White Knight (Shadow):** The shadows of the rogue's arc are all about tempting the rogue with stability, while seeking to trap them in the process. For the white knight, this manifests as a character who seems to protect the rogue, but who really views them as a trophy. If the white knight successfully "conquers" the rogue, they won't hesitate to drop them back into the same negative situations they found them in.
- **The Dealer (Shadow):** Following along with the white knight, the dealer seeks to possess the rogue for their own benefit. Typically, this character promises the rogue money or safety in exchange for

providing some service. However, if the rogue gives in, the dealer will raise their demands more and more until the rogue ends up trapped with no escape.

- **An Echo (Shadow):** The last shadow of the rogue's arc is one that reminds the rogue of their own doubts and insecurities. This character parrots the rogue's failings and fears back at them, kicking them down when they're at their most vulnerable—even if they think they're doing the rogue a favor.
- **The Jailer (Herald):** The jailer arrives in the rogue's life with a warning: either escape now, or lose what little freedom you still have. This heralds the coming upheaval of the rogue's life, and is often what spurs them to begin their arc in the first place.
- **The Map (Herald/Shadow):** If it isn't the threat of a jailer that pushes the rogue to action, then it'll often be a map. This character shows up in the rogue's life with the promise of relief, power, and safety—exactly what the rogue has been looking for. Sometimes this isn't a character at all, but a literal treasure map! Either way, there is always a risk that the map morphs into a dealer or white knight as the rogue's arc unfolds.
- **The Town Mayor (Threshold Guardian):** We're back to the town mayor again, who serves the same role here as in the hermit's arc. This character holds a position of authority in the rogue's world, and thus the keys to the rogue's acceptance—*if* the rogue can prove themselves.
- **Polite Society (Threshold Guardian):** Polite society acts as the final threshold guardian of this arc. These are the characters the rogue is seeking legitimacy from, meaning their opinions and judgment is of the utmost importance. However, this doesn't always

mean polite society is right. Often, the rogue will have to overcome this guardian by learning to ignore it, thus stripping these characters of their power in the rogue's life.

The Lover's Arc

The lover's arc is all about learning to care for another person, even when doing so requires us to give up some of our own desires. Because of this, the lover's arc features a variety of interesting archetypes, some encouraging, some disruptive:

- **The Widow (Mentor):** The widow is an experienced character, one who has loved and lost and thus understands how fragile love truly is. As a mentor, the widow's job is to guide the lover as they accept that relationships require trust, sacrifice, and effort, even when things go awry.
- **The Maiden (Mentor/Ally):** In contrast, the maiden is the opposite of the widow. This character is young and naïve, not yet jaded by the world around them. They serve to remind the lover of how wonderful love truly is, helping them tap into the youthful joy that relationships can bring.
- **A Trusted Confidant (Ally):** The lover's primary ally comes in the form of a confidant, a close friend the lover can confide in as their relationship unfolds. Often, this confidant will act as a matchmaker for the lover and their future partner, though some confidants are simply a supportive shoulder to lean on.
- **Temptation (Shadow):** Temptation is a powerful force in the lover's arc, manifesting as alluring

characters who try to pull the lover away from their partner. This temptation isn't strictly physical either. Though your lover might be tempted by lust or attraction, this shadow can also come with the promise of acceptance by your character's family, society, or friends. If their relationship with their partner is struggling under the judgment of others, this might be a difficult offer to pass up.

- **Dark Whispers (Shadow):** Meanwhile, dark whispers are all about magnifying the lover's fears. This character is one who encourages the lover to doubt their relationship or their ability to love, either out of a misguided desire to protect them or perhaps a purposeful attempt to disrupt their life. Either way, the lover must learn to ignore or outright reject this character's influence if their relationship is to succeed.
- **The Family (Shadow/Threshold Guardian):** The last of the lover's potential shadows, the family is an interesting archetype. These characters could be your lover or their partner's literal family, but they could also be society at large. Either way, they question the lover's relationship. In doing so, they drive a wedge between the lover and their partner, acting as both a powerful shadow and a threshold guardian to overcome.
- **Their Partner (Herald):** In this arc, the herald is almost always the lover's partner themselves! This character arrives in the lover's life, shaking them out of stasis and upending their world. That first spark of attraction is a power thing, and acts as the perfect warning of all the adventures to come.
- **The Best Friend (Threshold Guardian):** Finally, the best friend is a close ally of your lover's partner.

They want what's best for their friend and thus need to deem the lover worthy before giving the relationship their blessing. In doing so, they coax the lover's partner to embrace the lover, easing the lover's path as they continue to pursue a relationship.

The Mother's Arc

Next, the mother's arc is all about accepting the challenges of leadership. Naturally, that means this arc comes with a lot of important allies. The mother needs a community they care about to spur them to action, while also making the hardships they face worth the effort:

- **The Grandmother (Mentor):** Often an extension of the mother, the grandmother is someone who has already experienced a mother's arc of their own. This gives them the wisdom and perspective needed to teach the mother important lessons about leadership, as well as offer practical support along the way.
- **Their Children (Ally):** Next, the children are a key group of characters who give the mother a reason to fight—and honestly, I probably should have chosen a less obvious name. These are the mother's main allies, who support the mother and encourage them (either directly or indirectly) to take responsibility for their world.
- **A Beloved Daughter (Ally):** Alongside their other children, the mother will usually have a favorite. This beloved daughter reminds the mother of their younger self, causing them to feel fiercely protective. As the mother struggles through their arc, the beloved daughter will be there to show them how far

they've come, and just how much they could lose if they fail.

- **Blood Brothers (Ally):** Last of the mother's potential allies, the blood brothers are a group of characters who fight alongside the mother, and often provide one of the most vital sources of support throughout their arc. Unlike the children or even the beloved daughter, these characters aren't seeking protection. Instead, they believe in the mother's cause, and are willing to do whatever it takes to see that cause realized.
- **The Warlord (Shadow):** Fighting against the mother is the warlord. This shadow is a powerful force, one who seeks to destroy and consume the mother's world for their own gain. Though the warlord is often an outsider, they can also be a rising figure from within the mother's community. Either way, they come into direct conflict with the mother, and are often the final hurdle the mother has to face to complete their journey.
- **The Father (Shadow/Threshold Guardian):** If they don't face a powerful warlord, the mother might instead fight against the father. Unlike the warlord seeking to pillage and destroy, the father is simply weak or misguided. Their rule over their world is decaying, and the mother is trying to fill that void. However, the father doesn't see it that way. They cling to control, putting a difficult hurdle between the mother and their goals. This archetype is closely tied to the leader's arc.
- **The Winds of Change (Herald):** The winds of change are a rather nebulous herald, largely because almost anything could spark the Catalyst of the mother's arc. Whatever these winds are, they reveal

the growing unease in the mother's world, alerting them to just how vulnerable their community truly is.
- **The Court Jester (Threshold Guardian/Shadow):** Rounding things out, we have a final archetype, one that could act as either a threshold guardian or a shadow. This character might seem weak on the surface, but they hold surprising sway over the old leadership of the mother's world. Because of this, they're out to test the mother. If the mother comes up short, the court jester will do everything they can to undermine them from within.

The Leader's Arc

Continuing from the mother's arc we have the leader, whose journey is all about relinquishing power to the next generation. Along the way, their supporting cast will test them at nearly every step:

- **The Loyal Advisor (Mentor):** The leader's oldest ally, the loyal advisor is basically what they sound like. This character never loses faith in the leader, but they also represent the status quo. Though they strive to guide the leader where they can, they often don't have the foresight to realize the leader's time is up.
- **The Heart (Mentor):** A mirror to the adviser, the heart is a character who connects with the leader on an emotional level and coaxes them to accept their loss of power. Typically, they'll be an outsider, meaning they can speak to the leader as an equal—not as a subject.
- **The People (Ally):** The leader's greatest ally will

always be their people. This is the backbone of their community and the reason they confront their story's core conflict in the first place. However, the people are fickle, and the leader must take care to retain their trust.

- **The Rotten Throne (Shadow):** A common shadow in this arc is the rotten throne, which represents the decay of the leader's own kingdom. Sometimes, this decay manifests within the leader themselves, often in the form of their declining health or mindset, though it can certainly be embodied by a specific character.
- **The Rebel Leader (Shadow):** Alongside the rotten throne, the rebel leader is a shadow who stokes dissatisfaction among the people. This character rejects the leader's rule, rallying the people behind them either for good or ill. As a result, they weaken the leader's position, forcing the leader to adapt quickly if they want to survive.
- **The Night Guard (Herald):** The night guard is a watchful force who sounds the alarm that the leader's world is under threat. They might be a literal guard, but they could also be a doctor warning of a growing illness or an accountant realizing the company is broke. Either way, they alert the leader to the conflict they're about to face.
- **The Protégé (Threshold Guardian):** Finally, the protégé is who will ultimately succeed the leader. To complete their arc, the leader must prove themselves to this character by accepting them as their successor and nurturing their potential—or risk them transforming into a dangerous rebel leader.

The Elder's Arc

The elder's arc completes the life of your character, following them as they face the reality of their own mortality. In order to complete this arc, the elder will need to embrace their death—not as an enemy, but as a friend:

- **The Truly Ancient (Mentor):** The only mentor capable of teaching the elder is one even older than themselves. This mentor has already faced death, before returning to guide those who come after them. Often, this character will be a spirit, but they could be a physical person who has only died metaphorically. Either way, they have the spiritual wisdom needed to help the elder complete their arc.
- **A Younger Sister (Ally/Herald):** The younger sister represents the naïve child, hero, or heroine. This character comes to the elder for guidance or help, often alerting them to the rot threatening their world. In doing so, they give the elder something to fight for—as most elders become fiercely protective of their younger charges before their arc is over.
- **The Responsible One (Ally):** In contrast to the younger sister, the responsible one is another youthful character, but one with a bit more experience under their belt. This character is who the elder will eventually entrust their world to after they've accepted that their time is up. In some stories, the younger sister and the responsible one are one in the same.
- **The Gentle Nurse (Shadow):** The first of two shadows, the gentle nurse disguises a dark disease beneath their kind exterior. This shadow encourages the elder to grow numb, telling them to "make

themselves comfortable" and ignore the approach of death. In order to complete their arc, the elder will have to reject this shadow, actively facing their end rather than mindlessly decaying.

- **A Vicious Beauty (Shadow):** Meanwhile, the elder will also have to struggle against the vicious beauty, a character who rejects death and clings to their youth at all costs. In some ways, this character represents the negative elder, hurting others in order to preserve their own life or perhaps tempting the elder with false promises of immortality.
- **The Spectre of Death (Herald):** Closely linked to the spectre of death that heralds the hero's arc, this spectre is some omen or premonition that alerts the elder to the imbalance spreading through their world. This spectre could be a disease within the elder themselves, the threat of loss or change, or even a wider threat to their community.
- **Death Himself (Threshold Guardian):** Finally, we come to the only threshold guardian of the elder's arc —that being death itself. In order to complete their arc, the elder must face death and accept it, not as a dangerous shadow but as one more phase of life. If they succeed, they'll find the strength needed to complete their arc, while failure will bring their destruction.

The Redemption Arc

Last but not least, we have the redemption arc!

This is a unique arc, in that it focuses on a character who grows from a negative to positive arc. In the process, they'll realize just how destructive their past was, repent for those actions, and eventually gain forgiveness. This sets them up to face a variety of powerful supporting archetypes:

- **The Wise Uncle (Mentor):** The main mentor of the redemption arc, the wise uncle is some authority figure who sees your character's potential for growth. Throughout their journey, they coax your character to heal, either by sticking by their side, vouching for them to others, or even working from afar to obstruct their more destructive tendencies.
- **The Right Hand (Ally):** Meanwhile, the right hand usually understands that your character is harmful (or at least has some inkling), but remains loyal despite this. Beneath your character's harmful exterior, the right hand sees something worthwhile.
- **The Enabler (Shadow):** The enabler encourages your character's negative habits, either in order to exploit them for their own gain or due to their own flaws and weakness. In order to complete their arc, your character will have to reject the enabler's influence and realize they're wrong.
- **A Symbol (Shadow/Threshold Guardian):** Your character will also be confounded by someone who symbolized their inner struggle in the flesh. This shadow is typically the final test of your character's arc, meaning they cannot gain forgiveness without first defeating the symbol of their destructive past.
- **The Carrot (Herald):** At the start of their arc, your character will be pursuing someone (or something) in the form of the carrot. The arrival of this herald is what initially lures your character out on their journey hoping to soothe their internal wounds. Without the carrot, they likely would have remained in stasis forever.

- **A Gentle Child (Herald):** Meanwhile, the gentle child is your character's first chance to show their good side. This herald is weak and vulnerable, but also ignorant of your character's crimes. Though they rarely stick around for long, the way your character treats them will signal to your readers that their redemption arc is about to begin.
- **The Bishop (Threshold Guardian):** Finally, the bishop acts as the moral center of your story. This is a character your readers like and trust, meaning their judgment holds a lot of sway. As a result, your character will have to gain the bishop's forgiveness, proving that they've repented and thus giving their arc legitimacy in the eyes of your audience.

Lessons from Chapter Fifteen

Overall, these universal archetypes provide a great "big picture" view of your cast. From mentors to allies and shadows, you can clearly see how your supporting characters might take shape, depending on the specific secondary arcs your novel features.

You can even find examples of these archetypes in our past case studies! Morph is the loyal pet to Jim Hawkins, while Eris acts as an echo to Sinbad. Meanwhile, Mr. Andrews represents the family in Peter's lover's arc, while Captain von Trapp is the father in Maria's mother's arc. Though you won't find these archetypes in every story (again, these don't *have* to appear in this exact form), it's fun to see how these common patterns show up again and again in new and exciting ways!

This extends to variations on these arcs too.

In this chapter, I described these archetypes mostly in terms of the positive arc, but negative and flat arcs will have supporting casts of their own. The main difference will be the affect these archetypes have on your character.

For instance, the widow of a negative lover's arc might teach the lover to be bitter or afraid of loss, while the maiden ends up exploited or heartbroken, reinforcing their inner struggle. Meanwhile, the old friend of a flat hermit is often a fraught relationship, even though they're an ally. The hermit was driven into the wilderness due to their truth, and their old friend likely didn't support them, meaning it'll take time for that relationship to heal.

Whatever your character's unique arc is, don't be afraid to put interesting twists on these archetypes. No part of your story exists in isolation—these supporting archetypes just serve to prove that!

In the meantime, here are a few questions to help you apply what you've learned to your cast:

- Who among your cast will support and guide your character throughout their arc?
- Will your character have any close allies or friends?
- How will the shadows of your story obstruct your character?
- Will they ever have to prove themselves to some guardian or authority figure?
- Who or what heralds the start of their journey?

Once you've answered these questions, I'll see you in Chapter Sixteen!

16

WHO NEEDS AN ARC?

Throughout this book, we've been hyper-focused on the world of character arcs—so much so that I wouldn't blame you if you assumed every character in your novel needs an arc.

However, that focus hides a more complicated truth.

You see, only a small subset of your cast will actually warrant arcs of their own. On the surface, that might seem like a hard sell. As I've said repeatedly throughout this book, change is a critical part of writing cathartic stories, and character arcs are vital to crafting that realistic change.

So, what's the deal?

Well, character arcs do play a big part in creating compelling novels—but the reality is that not every character *needs* to change. This comes down to focus. Technically, every character you write is the hero of their own story, and could likely support an arc of their own with enough time and attention.

Yet, that doesn't mean that character will be your novel's focus. The random grocery clerk who sells your protagonist a bag of apples or the nice bus driver who takes them home might be important to your story in a practical sense, but that doesn't make them central to your novel. Instead, your hero, allies, and villains are, and thus they're the characters who warrant the attention a character arc requires.

Because of this, arcs are best reserved for major players in your novel like your protagonist and their key allies. In smaller stories, this often results in only one fully developed character arc—while even large, ensemble casts might only have four or five arcs. This raises an important question...

How do you know which of your characters deserve an arc of their own?

Dynamic, Round, or Background?

Sometimes, the answer to this question will be obvious. For instance, your protagonist will always have a character arc—they are the central focus of your novel, after all!

Beyond your novel's hero, a lot of this comes down to trusting your gut. Some members of your cast will call out to you, and the fascinating stories they have to tell will practically demand that you give them an arc. In other cases though, you may be less sure. You want your cast to feel vibrant and lively, but you also don't want to overwhelm readers with arcs that don't belong.

This is where the idea of dynamic, round, and background characters comes into play.

Dynamic Characters:

First, dynamic characters form the backbone of your novel.

These characters are those who undergo significant transformations throughout your story, shifting their worldview and beliefs as part of a character arc. As their journey unfolds, they'll face their inner struggle, learn some important truth, and change as a person—either for better or for worse. This ties in closely with your novel's plot. Without the initial spark that triggers their Catalyst (and the continuing pressure your plot provides), their arc would never happen in the first place.

Dynamic characters also tend to have a unique relationship with your readers.

Typically, these are the characters you'll want readers to identify with the most, meaning they'll often act as point of view characters. From your protagonist to other members of your core cast, these are the ones who capture your readers' hearts more than any others.

Round Characters:

Alongside dynamic characters, you'll also have a variety of round characters.

Round characters are those without arcs, but who are still fully formed, well-developed people. These characters will have clear story goals, flaws, fears, and motivations, but won't undergo a significant transformation over the course of your story. Instead, what makes them interesting are their personalities and actions. A character can still be integral to your novel without a character arc!

With that said, this doesn't mean round characters won't experience conflict or change. They might gain a new skill, earn some status, or discover a new perspective. The real difference here is that round characters aren't torn between an inner struggle and truth, meaning they don't change their deepest beliefs—otherwise known as an arc.

As an example, think of Princess Leia from the original *Star Wars* trilogy.

Leia is an undeniably interesting, imposing figure, one who plays a major role in the rebel cause. However, she also has no arc to speak of. Instead, she's a round character, complete with a distinct personality, a strong story goal, and her own challenges to overcome. This doesn't make her boring or lackluster! It just means she isn't the primary focus of the trilogy.

Background Characters:

Finally, your cast will also feature a wide variety of background characters.

These characters are those with little to no character development, sparse backstory, and a mostly utilitarian role in your novel. Many background characters can be summed up with a single word, such as naïve, funny, or aggressive—they might not even have a name. Because of this, they aren't meant to be your reader's focus. Though they serve an important purpose in your story, their job is to fill the gaps left by the rest of your cast.

This means background characters are mostly function over form. Though these characters will help you flesh out your worldbuilding and create obstacles within your plot, they're really there to get your story from point A to B without a ton of hassle.

Thanks to these three types of characters, you can hopefully see how your cast might come together. Though you'll likely have only a few dynamic characters, that doesn't mean your story won't also feature a variety of richly detailed round characters, as well as a few background characters to flesh things out.

This ends up looking something like this:

- **Dynamic Characters:** The focal point of your story, usually consisting of your protagonist and one or two other characters. These characters form your novel's backbone and undergo significant internal transformations throughout their journey.
- **Round Characters:** Members of your core cast who don't have full arcs, but who are still fully realized people with clear goals and desires. These characters create conflict, provide support, and add depth to your story.
- **Background Characters:** Finally, background characters are supporting cast members who are there purely for utility. They might get your hero from one place to another, highlight key worldbuilding, or progress your plot. While they likely have a few personality traits, they are not fully developed people.

How these numbers work in practice will of course depend on your novel itself. Flash fiction, novellas, and short standalone novels will often feature just a single dynamic character, or perhaps two at the most. Meanwhile, longer series, trilogies, or massive epics can support a wide variety of arcs. Ensemble casts often feature four, five, or even six dynamic characters, alongside a dozen or more round characters each with their own personalities.

Here are a few examples of this, based on the case studies from this book:

- ***Casablanca* (1942):** One dynamic character (Rick), four round characters (Ilsa, Victor, Major Strasser, and Captain Renault), and 12+ background characters.
- ***Legally Blonde* (2001):** One dynamic character (Elle), five round characters (Emmett, Vivian, Paulette, Brooke, Professor Callahan), and 12+ background characters.
- ***Star Wars: A New Hope* (1977):** Three dynamic characters (Luke, Han Solo, and Obi-Wan), four round characters (Princess Leia, C3-PO, Chewbacca, and Darth Vader), and 12+ background characters.
- ***Avatar: The Last Airbender* (2005):** Five dynamic characters (Aang, Zuko, Katara, Toph, Azula), a variety of round characters (Mai, Suki, Sokka, Iroh, etc...), and dozens of background characters.

Lessons from Chapter Sixteen

Ultimately, whatever arcs—and thus dynamic characters—you create, they all need to revolve around the same core conflict. While these arcs can be varied and unique, this will ensure they share some connective tissue, and thus deserve a place in your larger story.

If you're struggling with this, picture your cast.

If you had to categorize them, who in your novel would be dynamic, round, or background? This isn't a judgment call, and it doesn't mean one group is better or worse than the other. Plenty of readers grow to adore certain background characters (see Cabbage Man from *Avatar: The Last Airbender*), and round characters can still be the life of the party when needed!

By visualizing these categories, you simply get a better picture of the work you need to do. Your background characters can be simple and streamlined, while your round ones will demand a bit more love and care. Finally, your dynamic cast is where you should place your focus. If a character warrants this label, you'll need to put in a lot of work to craft their arc and ensure their journey feels complete.

So long as you balance these three groups, your final cast should more than capable of supporting your story!

In the meantime, here are a few questions to help you apply what you've learned to your cast:

- Which characters are your novel's focus?
- Do each of these characters undergo significant internal change throughout their story?
- What about characters who don't have arcs, but are still fully realized people?
- Are there any gaps in your cast that could be filled by background characters?

Once you've answered these questions, I'll see you in Chapter Seventeen!

17

STRIKING A BALANCE

For many writers, the idea of character arcs is tightly connected to their protagonist—and, that's great! Your protagonist is the central figure of your novel, and thus critical to its success. By crafting a solid arc to guide their story, it'll be that much easier to ensure they leave a lasting impact on your readers' minds.

Of course, this comes with a caveat.

Like I mentioned in the previous chapter, every character is the hero of their own story, and any character can have an arc. Though your novel might not focus on them quite as much as your protagonist, these other characters will still have their own suite of turning points, conflicts, and supporting archetypes behind them. Your leader might be confounded by a rebellious heroine, who might be mentored by a wise elder, all at the same time!

This is a big part of elevating your cast to the next level. Depending on the scope of your story, you might feature a single arc in the form of your protagonist. However, you could also have a whole suite of engaging character arcs—and those arcs need to work together.

To create the maximum emotional impact, every arc in your novel should complement the others, balancing their various transformations to create contrast, catharsis, and the illusion of a vibrant, interconnected world. So, to help you achieve this, let's explore how these unique character arcs might combine in your own novels.

Pairing Your Characters

Though I'm only mentioning this now, you've hopefully noticed a few extra character arcs present in this book's case studies. Many of the best stories include a variety of arcs, both primary and secondary, that work in concert to create a multi-layered adventure.

Take *Treasure Planet*, for example.

Though we focused on Jim's coming of age arc, that movie also featured a positive rogue's arc in the form of Silver—while a story like *Red River* is built around both a positive leader's arc and a positive mother's arc. While these kinds of pairings are far from a requirement, they are common in a wide range of stories, and add another layer of depth that a standalone arc can't always provide.

So, how does this work?

Well, the specifics obviously vary from story to story, but there are a few common pairs you're likely to run into. These pairs are closely connected, and each of their journeys directly shape the other. We'll start with primary arcs:

- **Positive + Negative Arc:** In this pairing, your novel will feature both a positive and negative arc character, each focused on a similar inner struggle. This pairing serves to create contrast. As each character progresses through their arc, one will learn and thrive, while the other will double down and decay—allowing readers to see the consequences of their arcs in real time.
- **Flat + Positive Arc:** Meanwhile, flat arcs are often paired with a corresponding positive arc. Because the flat arc is focused on a character sharing their truth with others, this gives them an outlet for that mission. The more the positive arc character grows and evolves, the more confident the flat arc character becomes in their truth, and vice versa.
- **Failed Flat + Negative:** Of course, not all flat arc characters succeed. In these cases, their corresponding pair will be a negative arc, someone who rejects their truth and succumbs to their inner struggle even as the flat arc tries to guide them. The result will be the negative character's downfall, and a painful failure for the flat character.

Alongside these primary arc pairs, you might also notice a variety of common secondary arc pairs. These work in much the same way, with one character's secondary arc shaping and encouraging the other's:

- **Lover + Lover:** Probably the most obvious of these, lovers tend to come in pairs. Often, you'll have a positive lover and a corresponding flat lover, for the reasons we discussed earlier. Either way, as each lover learns to embrace the other, both characters progress along their arc.

- **Mother + Leader:** Another (somewhat) self-explanatory pair, the mother and the leader tend to go together. As the leader faces the increasing unrest in their community, the mother steps up to fill their place. This pushes the mother to prove themselves to the leader, and for the leader to accept the mother as their heir.
- **Coming of Age + Leader:** Filling a slightly different niche than the mother, the coming of age character often has to break away from a leader's grasp. As they establish themselves as an independent adult, this creates a crisis for the leader, forcing them to recognize that their rule is over. If all goes well, the leader will accept the child as an equal, and the child will prove themselves worthy.
- **Mother + Coming of Age:** Of course, some leaders represent nothing but decay. In these cases, a mother character is often called to take power in order to shelter a younger coming of age character. Though the "father figure" is intent on controlling this child, the mother realizes it's time for them to grow up, completing their arc while facilitating the other character's coming of age.
- **Hermit + Hero/Heroine:** Because the hermit is an outsider, they're often paired with a corresponding hero or heroine. This character has been sent away from home, where they discover the hermit. In the process, the hermit teaches them about the many wounds of the known world—while the hero or heroine coax the hermit to forgive the past.
- **Rogue + Hero/Heroine:** Similar to the hermit, rogues pair nicely with heroes as well. In these cases, the hero or heroine act as a key ally in the rogue's arc,

while the rogue helps support and challenge them as they pursue their reward.

- **Redemption + Chosen One:** A key part of the redemption arc is forgiveness, specifically the forgiveness of some positive figure. Often, this role is filled by a chosen one, whose destiny gives them moral authority within their community. Meanwhile, the redemption arc character tests and obstructs the chosen one, forcing both character to learn and grow as they slowly progress through their arcs.
- **Elder + Everyone Else:** Finally, the elder's arc is heavily dependent on guidance. Because of this, elders often act as mentors to younger characters, especially (but not limited to) chosen ones, coming of age characters, heroes, and heroines.

This balancing act is especially apparent when it comes to your protagonist.

Though these pairings can occur between any characters in your novel, your protagonist is the central figure of your story—meaning their relationships will get the most time in the sun. This opens the door to a lot of interesting conflicts, and thus plenty of other arcs to challenge and support them!

Case Study: Aragorn, Frodo, and Gandalf

If you have even a passing knowledge of the fantasy genre, you're likely familiar with JRR Tolkien's *The Lord of the Rings* —or at least the tropes of *The Lord of the Rings.*

This trilogy of novels has spawned everything from games to movies and TV shows, and defined much of modern fantasy in the process. It tells the tale of a treacherous quest to destroy the One Ring, the source of the Dark Lord Sauron's power. In order for the land of Middle-earth to be healed, Sauron's rule must end, and the true king of men must return; no easy task with the Dark Lord's armies breathing down your neck!

All of this sets us up for an epic adventure, one focused on three major characters:

- **Frodo Baggins:** The first of two protagonists, Frodo follows a flat hero's arc. He already knows his truth at the start of his story, and instead sets out to heal the wounds of his world. As bearer of the One Ring, his ability to remain uncorrupted is key—both to his mastery of the unknown, and to the eventual salvation of Middle-earth.
- **Aragorn:** The second protagonist of the series, Aragorn is destined to rule as heir to the throne of Gondor. This leads to two interesting arcs. On the one hand, he follows a chosen one's arc, struggling to live up to his fate. Meanwhile, he also follows a mother's arc. He's forced to take charge and guide his allies to victory, eventually allowing him to embrace his role as both mother and chosen one.
- **Gandalf:** Finally, Gandalf isn't a protagonist in this story, but he is an important mentor character, as well as an excellent example of the flat elder's arc. Throughout the trilogy, he faces his death, sacrifices himself to protect his friends, and is resurrected. Through this, he not only teaches the rest of the Fellowship, but transcends life along the way.

When combined, these three characters (and their corresponding character arcs) form the backbone of this story.

While Frodo's quest helps inspire and encourage Aragorn to fulfill his role as a mother, Aragorn also fights to facilitate Frodo's journey into the unknown. Meanwhile, Gandalf guides them both through his elder's arc, providing the wisdom they need to face the challenges ahead.

Of course, how these arcs play out look a bit different for each character. Because Frodo and Aragorn are protagonists, their arcs take center stage, acting as a central pillar of each book. Still, Gandalf isn't entirely sidelined. Though his journey is more subtle, he still undergoes a clear elder's arc, facilitating the positive character arcs of his younger companions.

This makes *The Lord of the Rings* an excellent example of how your cast could balance each other. Though they'll all be following their own unique journeys, that doesn't mean their arcs won't matter to those around them!

Conflict, Foils, and Mirrors

With that example in mind, there are two final things you'll want to consider when building your cast:

Conflict and foil characters.

You see, one of the best ways to inject some extra spice into your cast is to give your characters conflicting story goals and arcs. This immediately pits your cast against each other, even if they would otherwise agree on most things—thus encouraging stakes, conflict, and tension.

For instance, say your protagonist is a chosen one, striving to prove themselves as they learn to master the magical powers they're destined to wield. However, you also have a bitter hermit, someone who has been hurt by those same powers.

As you can probably guess, this hermit won't see eye-to-eye with your protagonist—triggering a boat-load of conflict when that chosen one shows up on their doorstep asking for guidance. Rather than embrace your protagonist with open arms, your hermit character might insist on burying their knowledge of your chosen one's destiny, causing the two to battle back and forth as their conflicting perspectives butt heads. Eventually, this opens the door for both characters to grow. While your hermit teaches your chosen one to respect the true weight of their powers, your chosen one can help the hermit forgive the wounds of their past.

It's these deeply connected journeys that give your cast the appearance of a living, breathing world. After all, nobody is an island. Like it or not, our actions affect the people around us, while their lives affect us in turn. Sometimes these relationships are positive, but they don't have to be. Either way, our interactions with our community say a lot about us as people, and often determine the lessons we learn.

This is where foil characters comes into play.

If you've heard this term before, it's likely in the context of foil scenes, which are scenes in your novel that mirror earlier events in your story. This is a big part of creating catharsis. Not only are foil scenes often some of your story's most intense moments, but they also highlight just how much your novel has changed due to the events of your plot.

Meanwhile, characters arcs can have foils too! I hinted at this a bit when we talked about common primary arc pairings earlier—specifically the positive and negative arc. As the positive arc character learns and grows, the negative arc character withers and decays, mirroring each other's experiences and thus creating a foil.

So, what goes into a foil character?

Well, for starters, foil characters don't always need their own character arcs. You can certainly foil a dynamic character with a round character, simply by having both focus on the same goals or experiences. However, many of the best foils are based on opposing arcs. In these cases, both characters will need all the hallmarks of a well-developed character arc:

- A powerful inner struggle
- A corresponding truth
- A clear story goal

As an added element unique to foil characters, these three pieces should be linked. They might have the same inner struggle, but as one character overcomes it, the other succumbs to it. Alternatively, they could have opposite struggles, but discover the same truth. Or, perhaps they share a common story goal—at least on the surface.

This is another place where common character arc pairs become useful. Beyond the obvious positive/negative pair, I encourage you think hard about the kind of arcs you give your two foil characters. Some arc pairings work naturally as foils, such as the hermit and hero, or even the rogue and chosen one. You could also give the characters the same secondary arc, but opposing primary arcs. The possibilities are endless!

In the end, this doesn't have to be dramatic, and foils certainly aren't a requirement. Plenty of subtle foil pairings become fan favorites, like the aloof Sherlock Holmes and the down-to-earth John Watson. Whatever your ideal foil pairing looks like, this is just one more way to add a bit of spice to your novel.

Lessons from Chapter Seventeen

It's easy to neglect your cast in favor of just one or two main protagonists—but, no matter how tempting that may be, your cast deserves attention too.

These are the characters who will add richness and depth to your protagonist's story, even if their arcs are subtle (and even if they don't have an arc at all). By picking journeys and personalities that complement one another, you'll elevate your novel to a whole new level. After all, no part of your novel happens in isolation! Every decision your characters make will have ripple effects, shaping not only the rest of your cast, but your plot too.

Speaking of plot, this is one thing we've mostly neglected throughout this book.

Plot has a big role to play in your novel, but it doesn't exactly fall under the umbrella of "character development." Despite this, your plot will have a major impact on your cast, especially when it comes to their arcs. From crossroads to story structure, we have a lot of plot-related ideas to explore—but, I'll save those for the next chapter.

In the meantime, here are a few questions to help you apply what you've learned to your cast:

- Does your story include multiple characters with their own arcs?
- How do these arcs affect one another?
- Do your characters have any conflicting goals, desires, or beliefs?
- Could any of your characters benefit from a corresponding foil character?

Once you've answered these questions, I'll see you in Chapter Eighteen!

18

THE MYTH OF PLOT VS. CHARACTER

Though there are two sides to every story, many writers end up stuck on one or the other.

In the world of writing, plot and character are often treated like isolated planets. They never touch or come into contact, and though they might orbit each other, they couldn't be more different. Plot is active, dramatic, and explosive—while character is seen as sedate, introspective, and often "literary."

Because of this, writers often feel pressured to pick a side.

You might be a plot-focused writer or a character-focused writer, but rarely a little of both. In my case, I started out firmly in the realm of character. Early in my writing career, I would spend days tinkering with backstory, personality, names, and arcs, though I had no idea how to weave those arcs into a proper story. Without some plot to put them in, my characters withered away, driving me in endless circles as I tried to figure out what I was doing wrong.

Luckily, my writing skills have grown over the years, though I've never forgotten just how lost I felt in those early days.

That's the real problem with the plot-focused or character-focused approach—plot and character are inseparable!

This is why it's time for us to shift focus.

By now, you should be confident in your understanding of character arcs, but you might still be unsure how those arcs interact with the rest of your novel. We've touched on a few plot-related concepts, but only in passing. So, before we wrap up this book, we need to take a moment and explore the other side of the writing world.

An Inner and Outer Journey

Something you might have caught in earlier chapters is that your characters face a handful of crossroads throughout their arc. These crossroads take shape as their Catalyst, Turning Point, Regression, and Choice, combining together to fundamentally shift who they are as a person.

You hopefully *also* noticed that these crossroads rely heavily on your plot.

For instance, your character's Catalyst triggers the start of their arc, but it also forces them to engage with your novel's core conflict. This is what shakes up their life, setting the stage for their story. This change eventually culminates in the Turning Point, where your character will embrace their truth for the first time and gain a key victory—along with all the allies, tools, and skills that come with it. Finally, the Regression appears to be a painful failure, while the Choice determines both the outcome of their arc and the outcome of your story.

This means your characters' arcs are tightly connected to your plot. As your plot unfolds, it'll test and challenge your characters, teaching them important lessons as they struggle to achieve their story goal. Slowly but surely, these lessons will change their behavior and beliefs, while also changing how they interact with your plot.

When combined, this creates a powerful symbiotic relationship, one built on two dual journeys:

- **The Inner Journey:** A compelling inner life, where your character faces internal struggles and obstacles that leave them meaningfully different by the end of your novel. This is shaped by their identity, backstory, inner struggle, truth, story goals, and character arc.
- **The Outer Journey:** An engaging outer conflict, where your character fights against external challenges in pursuit of some larger goal. This is where they'll prove their transformation through action, making this the domain of your plot.

The inner journey is fairly self-explanatory, and has been our main focus throughout this book. However, the outer journey also its own role to play. Not only will it ensure your character remains active in your plot, but it'll also show readers how they're changing through their actions. For every decision they make, readers will learn a little more about their beliefs and goals, painting a vibrant picture as that character slowly transforms.

To tell the best possible story, you'll need to balance both of these dual journeys.

NOTE: The outer journey is something I covered extensively in *Write Your Hero,* so I don't plan to recap everything here. If you'd like to delve deeper into that side of your story, I recommend starting there.

Character Arcs vs. Story Structure

One of the great things about the inner and outer journey is that they're both shaped by common frameworks—specifically character arcs and story structure.

By now, you should be well acquainted with your characters' arcs, but the concept of story structure might still feel vague. Fortunately, these structures fulfill a similar role to character arcs. While arcs act as a framework for crafting strong characters, story structures provide a series of turning points and phases to help you create powerful plots.

Like arcs, this also means there are a lot of story structures to choose from, far more than we can realistically cover here. Still, I do want to show you how arcs and structure interact, as well as how they link your characters' inner and outer journeys. We'll be looking at one story structure in particular: the Three Act Structure.

This is one of the most popular story structures out there, as well as one of the most common.

Originally developed as a tool for Ancient Greek playwrights, the Three Act Structure has gone on to shape just about every aspect of modern storytelling, from movies and shows to novels. As the name implies, all of this is based on three phases, called acts:

- **Act 1 (Setup):** Starting off, this act is all about setting the stage. Here you'll introduce your characters,

establish their flaws and goals, and create a baseline for judging their growth. Eventually, this will culminate in a major turning point, where your plot (and core conflict) will kick into gear.
- **Act 2 (Confrontation):** Next, Act 2 forms the bulk of your novel. This is where your cast will face challenges, learn key lessons, and slowly come to grips with your story's conflict—culminating in a major turning point towards the middle of your story. Your characters will also face a moment of darkness, acting as one last hurdle between them and their truth.
- **Act 3 (Resolution):** Finally, once your cast recovers from the painful blow that ends Act 2, they'll enter Act 3. This is their final chance to face your core conflict, completing their adventure in a rousing finale that brings your plot to a close. As the dust settles, readers will get one final glimpse into their new life before you say "the end."

Alongside these acts, the Three Act Structure also includes a variety of story beats, referred to as plot points. These five form the backbone of this structure:

- **The First Plot Point:** Marking the end of Act 1, this is where your plot truly begins. By this point in your novel, you've introduced your core conflict and set your story into motion. Now, your characters will make some choice that embroils them in this conflict, triggering a point of no return.
- **The Midpoint:** Halfway through your novel, you'll come to the next turning point of your story. Here your characters will face a major challenge and succeed, equipping them with the confidence and

skills needed to take control of your plot. From here on out, they'll play an active role in your novel's conflict, rather than just reacting to the events around them.

- **The Third Plot Point:** This leads to a dark moment for your cast, where all of their plans fall apart. They underestimated your core conflict and were ultimately foiled by their inner struggles. The result is a harsh downfall, one your characters will have to learn from if they're to recover. The pace of your story speeds up from here, leading to a tense conclusion.
- **The Climactic Moment:** Next, your Climactic Moment is the true finale of your story. This is where your characters—primarily your protagonist—will make the decisions needed to resolve your core conflict, or succumb to their deepest flaws. Depending on their choice, this will determine the outcome of your plot.
- **The Resolution:** Last but not least, readers will get to see the aftermath of your story. Here you'll show them the long-term effects of your plot, as well as what life might look like for your cast now that their journeys are over.

You might notice that these acts and plot points sound somewhat familiar, and that's because each of them correspond to one of the eight phases of arcs we discussed back in Chapter Four. This is no coincidence. Because your plot and characters are linked, your character's arcs will unfold in concert with your plot, and thus alongside your story's structure!

Here's how these two sides match up.

- **The Beginning —> Act 1:** Both your plot and your character's arc will begin in their normal world, where you'll set the stage for everything to come. This is your chance to show why your plot matters to that character.
- **Catalyst —> The First Plot Point:** Next, it's time to light a fire! Here your character will make some choice that embroils them in your novel's core conflict, triggering their arc and your plot. From here on out, they can't easily go back to how things were.
- **The Reactive Phase —> Act 2:** Early in Act 2, your character will struggle to understand the scope of your core conflict. Their arc and your plot have only just begun, so they aren't quite ready to take charge.
- **Turning Point —> The Midpoint:** This culminates in a major test, where your character gains some tool, skill, or knowledge that pushes their arc into a new, active phase. This will also mark a shift in your plot. Your core conflict will take on a new angle, and your plot will begin to pick up speed.
- **The Active Phase —> Act 2:** Armed with more confidence, your character will develop a new plan for resolving your core conflict. However, not all is well. Their inner struggle is lingering, and your antagonist still holds a lot of power.
- **Regression —> The Third Plot Point:** Eventually this causes their plans to fall apart, leading to a painful defeat. This marks a dark moment for both your plot and their arc.
- **Choice —> The Climactic Moment:** After reflecting on their journey, your character will rise back up and make the decisions necessary to resolve your novel's conflict, proving their transformation and bringing

your plot to a close. Alternatively, some characters will fail here, leading to a negative outcome.

- **The End —> The Resolution:** Finally, you'll end with a glimpse of life after the dust settles. Your plot has wound down, and the results of your character's arc (and the conflicts they faced) are clear.

All of this ties back to the four crossroads I mentioned earlier—those being the Catalyst, Turning Point, Regression, and Choice. Each of these crossroads corresponds to one of the main plot points of the Three Act Structure, forming central pillars for both your core conflict and cast. The result is a tightly woven story, one where both your plot and characters evolve in sync. As your characters face key moments of change, so will your story itself, and vice versa.

This extends beyond the Three Act Structure too.

Though the Three Act Structure makes for an easy example, nearly all story structures—from the Hero's Journey to Freytag's Pyramid—line up with these eight stages. You might have to tweak a few events to create a perfect match, but the end result will be basically the same. As your cast transforms, so too will your plot.

Lessons from Chapter Eighteen

The link between your plot and cast might be obvious to some, but I'll never forget what a light bulb moment this was within my own writing life. When I first started to take my novels seriously almost a decade ago, I felt trapped beneath the "character-focused" side of this equation. Only after a lot of research and plenty of mistakes did I allow myself to let go of this identity and instead embrace just how inseparable plot and character truly are.

Where this overlap is extra obvious is with your protagonist.

Because your protagonist is the central character of your novel, they'll also be the one whose arc aligns most closely with your plot—or at least they should be.

Still, that doesn't mean the rest of your cast won't be affected by these dual journeys. Though their arcs might shift away from your story's structure, they'll still be deeply affected by the crossroads spread throughout your plot. I like to think of these as "hotspots." If both your protagonist, key allies, and your plot all reach a turning point at the same time, it'll create a powerful one-two punch for your readers. Though not a requirement, it's worth striving for when possible.

Ultimately, even if your side characters experience a more subtle arc than your protagonist, these principles remain the same. To create the best possible story, every piece should be connected!

In the meantime, here are a few questions to help you apply what you've learned to your cast:

- Which story structure do you plan to use as you write your novel?
- What major crossroads does your plot contain?
- How do these crossroads affect both your character's arc, as well as your plot?
- How do characters' journeys shape your novel's core conflict?

Once you've answered these questions, I'll see you in Chapter Nineteen!

19

HONORING YOUR VISION

When you think hard about your novel, I imagine a familiar picture starts to emerge.

You might see your protagonist standing tall on a windy ridge, or maybe you watch awestruck as a massive battle unfolds. Your story could be melancholy and subdued, or energetic and playful—or perhaps all you hear are the leaves of a dark forest crunching beneath your feet.

No matter what this image looks like to you, this is your vision for your novel.

Acting as the guiding star of your story, this vision is what got you excited to write in the first place. It's the core idea that drives your creativity and is thus what every aspect of your novel should be in service of. Of course, "should" makes this sound easy. As your story develops, you'll have dozens of forces pulling you in hundreds of directions, from writing rules and guidelines to shiny new ideas you can't help but explore. In the process, it's not uncommon to lose your original vision. That initial spark will get smothered by all the information clouding your mind, so that by the time you're halfway through your story, you'll hardly remember where you started from.

This is less than ideal, but it's also hard to avoid. Our visions tend to be fragile and amorphous, meaning it takes a lot of work to preserve them as we venture beyond that initial idea. So, what should you do? How can you stay true to your original vision, even as you develop your story?

Well, there is no perfect answer…

This is something even experienced authors struggle with, myself included. Still, it is a topic worth discussing. As you've gone through this book, you've likely gotten a lot of new ideas for where your characters might go—as well as a few uncomfortable realizations about what you've been doing wrong. In the process, I imagine your original vision began to slip, instead being replaced with the subconscious pressure of perfectionism and new ideas.

For the final chapter of this book, we need to return to that original vision.

Though we've talked a lot about frameworks and guidelines, these rules aren't the only part of writing a great story. Your vision is still a critical part of your novel! So, before I leave you to your devices, let's look at how to put everything you've learned into practice—while still honoring your vision at the same time.

How to Choose the Right Arcs

Before we get started, I want to explain what I mean by "vision" in a bit more detail.

Every writer's vision for their novel will be a little bit different, but whatever yours is, this is the core idea of your story. When you close your eyes and imagine your novel, this is what you see, smell, and hear. It encompasses the characters you want to create, the locations you want to explore, and the feelings you want to capture by the time you're through.

Obviously, this is highly personal.

For me, my vision for my stories is almost always based on a place. These places are the first thing I see when I start a new project, before any characters or plots come into view. Many writers I've worked with share a similar experience, while others focus on a specific person, event, or even phrase to spark their stories.

Whatever your vision is, it's easy for this to get lost as you expand your novel. In the context of this chapter, that "expansion" is all about arcs. We've covered a lot of character arcs throughout this book, from primary and secondary arcs, to hybrid and failed arcs—leaving you with more than enough options to choose from. This is undoubtedly overwhelming, but that's where your original vision comes in to save the day.

You should have answered a few dozen wrap-up questions at the end of each chapter, meaning you likely have a decent idea of the characters who will populate your story. Now, based on your notes, it's time to check your work. For each of the characters you plan to write, consider these questions:

- What struggles will that character face?
- Is their journey about their own growth or their effect on others?
- What lessons do you want them to learn?
- What kind of outcome will they experience?

- How should readers feel at the end of their journey?
- Is there a specific message or theme you want their arc to convey?
- How could their arc influence your other characters?
- What genre are you writing in, and what do readers of that genre expect?
- Which of the arcs from this book feel right for that character?
- What types of arcs are you most excited to explore?

As you go, make sure you're thinking carefully about your original vision. Do your answers align with the story you're trying to tell? Do they strike the right tone, and what do they say about your larger novel? If you're struggling with this, I encourage you to write your vision down. Putting your ideas on paper is a great way to reconnect with the origins of your story and preserve it as you move forward.

Another thing to consider is how these arcs resonate with your own lived experience.

It's common advice for writers to "write what they know," and while you shouldn't feel restricted by this, it's popular for a reason. Writing characters that mirror aspects of your own life can be extremely powerful, whether that comes in the form of common memories, emotions, or challenges. This lends a sense of realism to your characters, even if they look nothing like you or live in a world far different than your own. Because you understand their experiences on a deep level, you'll be much better equipped to tell their story with empathy and understanding.

Of course, you might not share much in common with your characters in the literal sense. You are a writer after all, and (though I'm not judging your life) I doubt you've ever sailed the high-seas as a pirate queen or wandered an alien space station as an intergalactic soldier. Still, human emotions are universal, and character arcs are built on universal patterns. Your pirate queen might be going through a complex mother's arc, meaning you can apply your own experiences with leadership as you tell their story. Perhaps your space adventurer is facing a redemption arc, allowing you to leverage your own struggles with forgiveness and regret to better understand their journey.

Whatever your life and the lives of your characters look like, the key is knowing when to trust your gut. Though this book has been focused on the frameworks and guidelines used to write strong characters, sometimes it's ok to bend the rules. Even if you have to return to the drawing board more than you might like, that extra work will be well worth it if it results in a novel that makes you proud.

Putting Arcs Into Practice

Choosing arcs for your characters is one thing—but applying them is another.

Once you've picked a series of character arcs you're happy with, you'll still need to put those arcs into practice. This will happen in a variety of ways depending on where you are in the writing process.

Outlining Your Novel:

Early on, you'll be busy brainstorming and planning your novel. This is where you'll flesh out your character's arcs and see how they might connect to the rest of your story.

Depending on the type of writer you are, this "planning" phase could culminate in a detailed story outline, or just a simple list of your characters' traits. Either way, this is your chance to do your homework. Use this time to test your characters' potential, ensure they have a clear inner struggle, and perhaps draft a few of the turning points of their arcs.

If you want to go further than this, you're certainly welcome to! I just wouldn't recommend skipping this step entirely.

> **NOTE:** If you'd like help building a story outline, *The Ten Day Outline* is worth looking into.

Writing Your First Draft:

From there, it's time to write your first draft—as well as put theory aside.

As counterintuitive as that might sound, the first draft isn't the place to obsess about the finer details of your story. During this process, you already have enough stress, writer's block, and perfectionism to deal with. If you've done your homework and developed at least a basic plan for your novel, all you need now is to trust your past self. Get your words on paper, accept that they might not be ideal, and give yourself permission to get things wrong. If you get stuck at any point along the way, use the character arcs you planned earlier to help you move forward.

Revising Your Story:

With your first draft finished (and a relaxing writing break under your belt), you can return to the craft of writing.

Editing is the perfect time to dig deep into the members of your cast, refining and tweaking them until they practically jump off the page. If you feel a specific character isn't as strong as they could be, their arc is a great place to start. Does their arc mesh with your plot? Are any of the eight phases missing, or otherwise incomplete? Do they not have a clear transformation at all?

While not all of your characters will have arcs, the ones that do need to pull their weight.

Working Through Feedback:

Finally, most writers will seek feedback on their novels in some form, whether that comes from beta readers, critique partners, or professional editors. Depending on who you work with, the type of notes you get could vary widely. Editors are usually good about identifying specific areas for improvement, while beta readers and critique partners are more vague. You might see statements such as "this character feels bland" or "I don't think they earned their victory."

Obviously, this type of advice is hard to parse through—which is where arcs become useful. As you review feedback from your readers, consider how their notes relate to your characters' arcs. If they aren't earning their victories, it could be that their inner struggle isn't clear or their Choice isn't definitive. Meanwhile, a bland character might need to face harsher conflicts or make stronger decisions throughout their journey.

Overall, the best way to ensure these stages go smoothly is to set yourself up for success early.

If you're just starting a new novel, you'll have plenty of time to plan your arcs and ensure they mesh with the rest of your story. In these cases, take your time and dig deep into how your characters could unfold. Usually, this will go a long way towards streamlining your first draft and reducing the kind of intense revisions you'll need to deal with down the road—though there will always be some surprises you can't avoid!

Of course, you might be reading this book while knee-deep in editing your draft. This is a trickier time to build complex arcs or transformations, but it's not impossible. If you're in this boat, my best recommendation is to pull back and get a bird's-eye view of your novel. The better you can see the bigger picture, the easier it'll be to bring your cast together.

Lessons from Chapter Nineteen

Ultimately, the result of character arcs is meaningful change.

Change is the lifeblood of good storytelling, as well as the secret sauce that leaves readers emotionally connected to our novels. Everything we've discussed throughout this book has been in service of creating this change. By combining what you've learned with a clear vision for your story, you should have all the tools you need to craft characters that feel alive in ways not unlike yourself.

It's been a long road to get here, but I hope you truly love the cast you've created!

In the meantime, here are a few questions to help you apply what you've learned to your cast:

- How would you describe your vision for your novel in a short paragraph?

- How does your cast connect to that vision, or further it in some way?
- Are you happy with the character arcs you've chosen?
- What experiences from your own life could help you better understand your characters?
- Are you excited about the cast you've created?

Once you've answered these questions, this book is officially complete!

WHAT COMES NEXT?

Over the last nineteen chapters, you've hopefully learned a lot about your cast. From their inner struggles to their supporting archetypes, unique journeys, and secondary arcs, these characters should be thriving in your mind—and perhaps on the page too!

All of this brings us to one final question…

What comes next?

Well, the answer is up to you. Depending on where you are in the writing process, there are many directions you could go in. You might be working on an outline, in which case you can use your new knowledge of arcs to build character profiles, develop your plot, and better understand your story. Alternatively, if you're trying to deepen your mastery of the writing craft—whether to help revise a draft or simply grow your skills—this is a great jumping off point for exploring even more about the world of character development.

Fortunately, no matter what your situation is, there are a few final ways I can help:

- ***Mastering Character Arcs* at a Glance:** First up, if you're looking for a quick way to review everything we've discussed, you'll find a handy "at a glance" section at the end of this book. This will include a short recap of each topic, along with the questions I asked at the end of each chapter.
- **Further Reading:** Next up is a further reading list. These are the books I found most helpful while developing my own knowledge of character development, so I recommend checking them out if you want to continue honing your cast. You'll also find a list of additional examples that didn't quite make it into the book, but that are still worth studying if you have the time!
- **My Other Books:** Alongside *Mastering Character Arcs,* I've also written a variety of other books on the writing craft. Whether you're looking to develop an outline, publish your novel, or become a better storyteller, I encourage you to give them a look!

If you'd like to stay in touch beyond this book, you can also find me over on my website. When I'm not busy writing books like these and getting lost in my own fictional worlds, I run **The Novel Smithy**, a site dedicated to giving writers the tools they need to create their dream novels.

Alongside regular articles on the writing craft, I also maintain a library of free resources built just for fiction writers, which you can check out here:

https://thenovelsmithy.com/library/

Finally, if you enjoyed this book, leaving a review would not only help me, but other writers like you. Reviews are how readers find the books they're looking for, so I'd be thrilled if you took a moment to share some honest feedback.

With that said, this book is officially complete!

Happy Writing,

Lewis Jorstad

JOIN THE LIBRARY!

Ever wish there was a library of resources built just for novelists? Well, guess what—there is!

Check out the **Novel Smithy Resource Library** and grab your **FREE Character Creation Workbook**.

https://thenovelsmithy.com/library/

ABOUT THE AUTHOR

Lewis Jorstad is a writer, author, and book coach, a lover of reading and travel, and a child at heart living in central Virginia. He hopes to visit every country in the world before he dies, but for now he spends his time teaching up-and-coming writers the skills they need to create compelling, successful novels.

You can find more of his work over at **The Novel Smithy:**

https://thenovelsmithy.com/

MASTERING CHARACTER ARCS AT A GLANCE

If you need a reminder of the topics we covered throughout this book, here they are in an easy-to-reference format:

CH 1: It's All About Change

Character arcs are the internal transformations your characters experience as they move through your story. These arcs are an important tool for writing cathartic novels, and will be our focus throughout this book.

- How would you describe your character's story in a few sentences?
- What failures will they experience along the way?
- How do they evolve and change as their journey unfolds?
- How do these changes affect them and the world around them?

CH 2: Gathering the Pieces

Well-written arcs build on a variety of elements, from a strong inner struggle to a powerful truth, compelling core conflict, and interesting backstory. When combined, these form your character's foundation.

- What harmful belief is holding your character back at the start of their story?
- What lesson will they need to learn in order to overcome that belief?
- How do their identity and backstory lay the groundwork for their inner struggle?
- How will your core conflict force their life to change?

CH 3: The Importance of Motivation:

It's easy to forget that our characters need a reason to engage with our plots—beyond just "that's how the story goes." This reason will be their story goal, the central motivation or desire that drives them to take action.

- What is your character's primary motivation throughout their story?
- Does this motivation change over time?
- Will they have to struggle between multiple conflicting story goals?
- How does this story goal get them involved in your novel's core conflict?

CH 4: The Two Types of Character Arcs

Character arcs come in two main forms: primary and secondary arcs. These two types of arcs combine to form nuanced, layered characters, all based on a simple eight-part structure.

- What key turning points do you already have in mind for your character, if any?
- What major event could trigger their arc?
- How will your plot test and challenge them as their story unfolds?
- What choice will they eventually make to prove they've changed as a person?

CH 5: Positive, Negative, and Flat

Positive, negative, and flat arcs are the most common types of character arcs in fiction, and for good reason. These three primary arcs provide the perfect baseline for understanding your character's overarching transformation.

- What does your character's life look like at the start of your story?
- How does this change by the end?
- Do they learn the right or wrong lessons during their journey?
- Is their story more about their own internal change or their effect on the world around them?

CH 6: What If They Fail?

Believe it or not, not all character arcs get a clean ending. These "failed arcs" follow your character as they undeniably evolve and change, but ultimately end their story stuck in stasis.

- Does your character end their story stuck between their truth and inner struggle?

- What traps them in this state of limbo?
- Do you plan to continue their arc in the future, or is this their true ending?
- How will you create catharsis for your readers, despite this failed arc?

CH 7: The Hero and the Heroine

The hero and the heroine were some of the first secondary arcs I studied as a young writer. Both arcs tell a classic story —though each from a slightly different perspective.

- Does your character leave their known world behind and venture into the unknown?
- If their arc focused primarily on physical mastery or internal wisdom?
- Do they eventually make the choice to return and help their community?
- How will they ultimately earn the title of hero or heroine?

CH 8: The Problems With Destiny

Growing up is a complicated time, and one we'll all have to experience. Meanwhile, fate, destiny, and prophecy make this process more difficult. This is where two secondary arcs come into play: the coming of age arc and the chosen one's arc.

- Will your character have to leave behind their child world and enter adulthood?
- How does their child world restrict them early in their character arc?
- Is their journey about facing their destiny and the many challenges that come with it?

- If so, how can you ensure they earn their victories, rather than having success handed to them?

CH 9: Surviving in the Wilderness

By far my favorite secondary arcs, the hermit and the rogue reject the classic hero mythos. Rather than set out into the unknown to protect their community, these characters start their stories alone in the wilderness, or perhaps trapped on the edges of the human world.

- What is your character's role in society when their arc begins?
- Are they isolated in the wilderness, or are they stuck somewhere along the edge?
- How does this impact their relationships with the people around them?
- What event (or events) could eventually bring your character back into the fold?

CH 10: Learning About Love

Love is a complicated thing, one ripe for interesting and compelling conflicts. Naturally, this lends itself to character arcs too—specifically in the form of the lover's arc!

- Does your character's internal transformation center on their relationship with another person?
- What choice or decision triggers that relationship (or some change in their existing relationship)?
- How does your lover's personality balance the personality of their partner?
- How will they eventually prove that they're ready for love?

CH 11: The Three Older Arcs

Alongside classic journeys of growth and identity, you'll also find stories that focus on older characters. These characters are those who struggle to bear the burdens of leadership, relinquish power to the next generation, or even accept their own deaths.

- Does your character struggle to take on the burdens of leadership throughout their story?
- Are they already in a position of power when their arc begins?
- Will they have to accept their own death to resolve your novel's core conflict?
- Do they have any younger arcs that complement their journey?

CH 12: Redeeming Your Characters

When it comes to redeeming your characters, your biggest challenge will always be your readers. Though *you* might forgive your character, readers are much more stubborn, meaning you'll need a carefully crafted redemption arc to win them over.

- What destructive belief haunts your character early in their story?
- What helps them realize they need to change?
- How will your character atone for their past actions?
- Will these sacrifices be equal in severity to the wrongs they've committed?
- Who will ultimately forgive your character and complete their redemption?

CH 13: Finding Their Path

Perhaps the best thing about character arcs is how they form layers! By combining primary and secondary arcs, you open up a whole world of interesting stories—from the flat hermit to the negative mother, positive elder, or failed heroine.

- Which primary arc is the best fit for your character?
- Will they have an additional secondary arc?
- Does their journey end in stasis, or do they get the catharsis they're looking for?
- How do these various arcs combine into a single, cohesive story?

CH 14: The Hybrid Arc

Of course, your characters aren't limited to just one primary/secondary combination. Though tricky to pull off, they could also follow a hybrid arc, one where multiple journeys of change happen in concert throughout their story.

- Does your character undergo multiple connected transformations?
- How do these transformations affect each other?
- Which of these arcs act as their foundational arc?
- What about their supplemental arcs?

CH 15: Five Supporting Archetypes

From mentors to shadows and threshold guardians, your characters will be supported by a wide variety of universal archetypes. These are a fantastic way to flesh out your novel's cast!

- Who among your cast will support and guide your character throughout their arc?
- Will your character have any close allies or friends?

- How will the shadows of your story obstruct your character?
- Will they ever have to prove themselves to some guardian or authority figure?
- Who or what heralds the start of their journey?

CH 16: Who Needs an Arc?

Though character arcs are important, not every character you write needs an arc of their own. This is determined by where they fall in three basic groups: dynamic, round, or background characters.

- Which characters are your novel's focus?
- Do each of these characters undergo significant internal change throughout their story?
- What about characters who don't have arcs, but are still fully realized people?
- Are there any gaps in your cast that could be filled by background characters?

CH 17: Striking a Balance

Much like your characters will be supported by universal archetypes, they'll also come into conflict with other characters—often with their own personal arcs.

- Does your story include multiple characters with their own arcs?
- How do these arcs affect one another?
- Do your characters have any conflicting goals, desires, or beliefs?
- Could any of your characters benefit from a corresponding foil character?

CH 18: The Myth of Plot vs. Character

Plot and character are intrinsically connected. Fortunately, the eight-part structure we've studied throughout this book is an easy way to see this in action!

- Which story structure do you plan to use as you write your novel?
- What major crossroads does your plot contain?
- How do these crossroads affect both your character's arc, as well as your plot?
- How do characters' journeys shape your novel's core conflict?

CH 19: Honoring Your Vision

Finally, no matter how many writing rules or guidelines you master, you'll always need some vision for your novel. This is the initial spark that inspired your story in the first place—meaning, before we wrap up, we need to take some time to honor your novel's origins.

- How would you describe your vision for your novel in a short paragraph?
- How does your cast connect to that vision, or further it in some way?
- Are you happy with the character arcs you've chosen?
- What experiences from your own life could help you better understand your characters?
- Are you excited about the cast you've created?

FURTHER READING

I consulted a lot of resources while writing this book, and while forming my own understanding of character development over the last decade. Though not an exhaustive list, here are a few sources I recommend checking out if you'd like to continue exploring your cast:

- *Wired for Story* — Lisa Cron
- *The Hero With a Thousand Faces* — Joseph Campbell
- *The Writer's Journey* — Christopher Vogler
- *The Heroine's Journey* — Maureen Murdock
- *Creating Character Arcs* — K.M. Weiland
- *The Emotional Craft of Fiction* — Donald Maass
- *Plot Versus Character* — Jeff Gerke
- *The Virgin's Promise* — Kim Hudson
- *The Heroine's Journey* — Gail Carriger
- *Romancing the Beat* — Gwen Hayes
- *Story Genius* — Lisa Chron

FURTHER EXAMPLES

I also referenced a variety of stories when choosing the case studies for this book, and (as much as I would have liked to include all of them) I eventually had to settle on just a few.

If you want even more examples of characters arcs in action, here are the other stories that inspired these journeys:

The Hero's Arc:

- Fa Mulan from Disney's *Mulan* (1998)
- Hiccup from *How to Train Your Dragon* (2010)
- Luke Skywalker from *Star Wars: A New Hope* (1977)

The Heroine's Arc:

- Moana from Disney's *Moana* (2016)
- Kiki from *Kiki's Delivery Service* (1989)
- Motoko Kusanagi from *Ghost in the Shell* (1995)

The Coming of Age Arc:

- Rose from *Titanic* (1997)
- Rapunzel from Disney's *Tangled* (2010)
- Simba from Disney's *The Lion King* (1994)
- Walter from *Secondhand Lions* (2003)

The Chosen One's Arc:

- Moses from *The Prince of Egypt* (1998)
- Po from *Kung Fu Panda* (2008)
- Aang from *Avatar: The Last Airbender* (2005)

The Hermit's Arc:

- The Beast from Disney's *Beauty and the Beast* (1991)
- Shrek from *Shrek* (2001)

The Rogue's Arc:

- Dallas from *Stagecoach* (1939)
- Qi'ra from *Solo* (2018)

The Lover's Arc

- Baby and Johnny from *Dirty Dancing* (1987)
- Elizabeth Bennet from *Pride and Prejudice* (2005)
- Betty Haynes from *White Christmas* (1954)
- Simon Basset from *The Duke and I* (2000)

The Mother's Arc

- Prince Albert from *The King's Speech* (2010)
- Kumatetsu from *The Boy and the Beast* (2015)

The Leader's Arc:

- James Bond from *No Time to Die* (2021)
- T'Challa from *Black Panther* (2018)

The Elder's Arc:

- Carl Fredricksen from *Up* (2009)
- Mother Gothel from Disney's *Tangled* (2010)

The Redemption Arc:

- Oskar Schindler from *Schindler's List* (1993)
- Harold Hill from *The Music Man* (1962)
- Darth Vader from *Return of the Jedi* (1983)

ALSO BY LEWIS JORSTAD

Ready to continue mastering your craft?

Check out Lewis' other books in The Writer's Craft Series, starting with Write Your Hero!

Made in the USA
Middletown, DE
04 December 2022